D0087446

FREEDOM OF THE MIND
IN HISTORY

FREEDOM
OF THE MIND
IN HISTORY

BY

HENRY OSBORN TAYLOR

GREENWOOD PRESS, PUBLISHERS
WESTPORT, CONNECTICUT

901
T24 f

Originally published in 1923
by Macmillan and Company, Ltd., London

m·R

Reprinted from an original copy in the collections
of the Brooklyn Public Library

First Greenwood Reprinting 1970

Library of Congress Catalogue Card Number 74-109861

SBN 8371-4352-7

Printed in the United States of America

TO

J. I. T.

v

UNIVERSITY LIBRARIES
CARNEGIE-MELLON UNIVERSITY
PITTSBURGH, PENNSYLVANIA 15213

PREFACE

In May 1920 I delivered the West Lectures at Leland Stanford Jr. University, selecting, as within the scope of the Founder's purpose, the subject indicated by my title-page. I spoke of the free action of the human mind through history, and tried to distinguish this agency from the grosser or more palpably determined factors shaping the fortunes of our race.

Doubtless the subject lacks definiteness. It is elusive and full of snares. Though I have since devoted a good three years to this small volume, and indeed most of my life in some way to its preparation, I feel it will be found logically reprehensible, and by no means free from inconsistencies. So is human nature. The full-minded man of many sympathies is a working union of inconsistencies. Assume him to be thoughtful and well read. Suppose that he loves literature and art ; that he has looked earnestly over the vista of history, and has carried his studies in various directions. Imagine him also drawn by religious feelings, or at least sympathizing with them ; and that he cares for the ultimate

vii

efforts of the mind in philosophy, and is interested in the inquiries of natural science. Not all these inclinations will move him at every moment with equal force. Perhaps his nature is never in perfect balance. His bodily cravings, his emotional impulses, his spiritual and intellectual aspiration, and his logic will not sit quietly together in the same little boat, and never rock it. Yet they are all his children, so to speak ; he cannot throw any of them overboard.

All the elements of our nature have a validity for us. We may disregard the pointings of none of them either in the conduct of our lives or in our search for truth. Indeed it is but a warped and partial being that will always act from one set of motives, always regard the same kind of data, and follow a like course of reason. The heroes of history, the chief workers in all the fields of human effort, even in their devotion to well-considered ends, have acted from feeling as well as under the rational direction of their minds. The heart's blood tells, and the impulsive devotions of the spirit, as well as the logic of the intellect.

Since our instincts and impulses, as well as our rational faculties, shape our perceptions and colour the world for each of us, they should all be admitted to our symposium. But a complete unison is scarcely to be expected in their report upon the truths of life. I have tried, however, to put their affirmations together as consistently as possible ;

and if the words seem here and there a little vague, well, one cannot always be precise in the broad matters of human contemplation.

I thank my friends, Mark Barr and Arthur C. McGiffert, President of Union Theological Seminary, for reading parts of the manuscript, and Professors Lawrence J. Henderson, of Harvard, and Frederick J. E. Woodbridge, of Columbia University, for reading the proof. The criticisms of such men naturally have been of great use to me.

HENRY OSBORN TAYLOR.

New York, *June* 1923.

CONTENTS

CHAPTER I

CHAPTER II

CHAPTER III

xi

CHAPTER IV

CHAPTER V

CHAPTER VI

CHAPTER VII

CHAPTER VIII

CHAPTER I

I

THEME AND METHOD

IN the perturbed and shaken world in which we move to-day, one may steady himself by contemplating the pointings of history. Antecedent courses of events bear upon the present social and political situation, and carry prophecies touching the prospects of mankind. The historical material is complex and voluminous. Its mass would tax encyclopaedias. Its diversity, its mottled hue, its dissidence and contrariety, its way of seething when constrained, and boiling over when compressed, embarrass the attempt to draw its total pertinency within the meshes of an argument. The entire significance of history will not be harnessed to the proof of any definite thesis. The day of such attempts has passed by, or is not yet.

Still I have a theme, if not a thesis. Realizing the insufficiency of my argument and the inconclusiveness of my proofs, I propose to supplement

B

one and the other with pointed illustrations from the quiver of history, in the hope of serving the time-honoured opinion which I hold, and which makes my theme. It is this : I conceive progress, by which I mean the increase of human well-being, to be the achievement of human faculty and the divine power. It seems to me to issue from the unfolding of the free energies of the human mind empowered and sustained by the creative and loving mind of God. Long lines of suggestive evidence, indeed I think the general course of history, may be adduced in favour of the human side of this proposition, which will form our main topic. Yet to many of us the human agency is unsatisfactory unless supplemented by some co-operative, or rather primordial, divine efficiency. The providence of God does not lend itself nowadays to demonstration. If real to us, it is so because we realize it religiously and have faith. This faith appears to be supported by broad inferences or inductions, which, however, are hard to make irrefutable.

Accordingly, with constant regard to the human part of our theme, I would refer first to the physical environment and animal antecedents of our race. The early manifestations of human faculties are next spoken of, all very briefly ; and then we are arrested by the troublesome question of the mind's free power. From this we endeavour to extricate ourselves as historians, leaving the physicists to whatever conclusions may be open to them. But thereupon, although no Samsons, we are caught in the toils of the equally impenetrable problem of the divine providence touching man. As to this, I can but give reasons for my own position, while at the same time pointing out the need to listen to the evidence of the chorus of human faculties, and admit the testimony of the whole man to our deliberation.

From these fundamental considerations we turn to the rôles of various peoples and great individuals in the drama of mankind's advance. Our search is for salient examples of the free action of the mind. No field is closed to us. Illustration may be sought in man's religious attitudes, or in the provinces of civil effort or intellectual creation. Political institutions and jurisprudence, art, philosophy, science, may be tapped at our discretion or indiscretion. It is better to look far and wide, since varied illustrations throw the broader light.

II

THE PLASTIC ENVIRONMENT

To-day all branches of science co-operate in the study of the character and behaviour of the physical world, and the stages through which it has reached its present state. Man is treated as part and parcel of this moving web. Science has drawn our gaze into novel vistas ; it has expanded to the infinite our thoughts of the labyrinthine universe of matter, energy, and life, whatever each of these may prove to be ; and close to us on every hand it has disclosed the unfathomable complexity of the infinitesimal. Withal, it has disciplined our minds. It has disposed us to recognize the course of natural law throughout our world, and indeed throughout the whole sidereal universe, which likewise appears to have reached its present state through natural or physical law. Such law means order and regularity of sequence, continuity indeed, as, for example, in the successive stages through which plants and animals have attained the forms which prevail at present. Our mind harnesses and dovetails these regularities of sequence, while our mental needs force us to clothe and energize them with some conception of causation. We try to analyze the specifically acting causes, and assign its effect to each ; or we may prefer to look to mutually enabling conditions, which appear to exercise efficiency or coercion.

So the whole world seems to move onward under law, possibly under necessity. Its laws are deemed to be inherent in matter, and in the natures of living organisms and the relations among them. Like other organisms, man seems the product of natural law—physical, chemical, biological, economic, even psychological and spiritual.

How or when organic life began is absolute mystery. The hypotheses still limp that would find its origin in some action of the inorganic elements. Yet the direct relationships are legion. Apparently some of the simplest and most abundant organisms, like the plankton or diatoms of the ocean, and to a large extent the world of plants, draw their nutriment directly from inorganic elements. The higher or more complex animal organisms require the inorganic air and water for their life and sustenance ; while for their more palpable food they prey upon other organisms, vegetable or animal, and thus draw indirectly upon the elements of the inorganic world.

Science has conjured up an astounding vision of the history of our earth, with its gaseous, molten formations, its changes, its inscrutable engendering of life's beginnings, and the ever marvellous progression of organisms, from amoebae and trilobites, through uncounted ages, through fishes, reptiles, monstrous dinosaurs, still through countless ages, to cleverer, more highly organized birds and mammals. Somewhere, or everywhere, in this progression of life, instinct and thought were obscurely dawning. It was a long, slow dawn, perhaps, until toward the hither end of this infinite record appeared animals nearing the shape of man. The record of the slow evolution of this organic form amounts only to suggestive fragments here and there.

Dependent on their physical environment, all living organisms are held within its enabling forces and controlling conditions. Their dependent and needful natures are fastened to their opportunities. The physical environment is the source from which these primarily animal needs must be satisfied. Very fundamentally, with consummated adaptability, the stability of the earth and the qualities of its inorganic elements—chief among them hydrogen, oxygen, and carbon, and their life-ensuring compounds, water and carbonic acid—permit the existence and make for the sustenance of life, make for its mobility and its complexity of development.[1]

Organism and environment : they seem distinct. Who would not distinguish the antelope from the grass it feeds on and the air it breathes ? Or even those blades of grass from the soil and atmosphere which furnish the elements of their growth ?

But it is not so clear. Our growing chemical and biological knowledge discloses the organism partaking of its environment and the environment interpenetrating the organism and becoming part of it : becoming not merely elementary material of its sustenance and growth, but part and parcel of its living substance—of its life. The oxygen of the air when breathed into an animal may still remain detectable as oxygen ; but, incorporated into the animal, its previous inorganic action seems transformed into a factor in the behaviour of a

[1] See L. J. Henderson, *The Fitness of the Environment* (New York, 1913) ; *ibid. The Order of Nature* (Harvard Univ. Press, 1917).

living organism. So the proteins of the palpable food-substances which are eaten. Once incorporate in the organism, their action changes and transcends the explanations of sheer physics or sheer chemistry.

The channels of interpenetration and transmuting of organism and environment are still unnumbered. Is not our weight part of the gravitation of the earth ? Organisms cannot be accounted for or described in terms of the physical laws applicable to the inorganic world. They are alive. Yet they cannot be separated without change from all that surrounds and penetrates and sustains them.[1]

Besides, the individual animal or plant is not simply itself, but a handing on, a continuance, of the species ; and the species is one long and vanishing recessional into a not merely cradling and sustaining, but a constantly insinuating and reciprocating environment. The species lives and functions in the individual. Individual, species, environment are and always have been in and of each other.

---

[1] " There is no sharp line of demarcation between a living organism and its environment. The persistence of the internal environment and its activities is, in fact, as evident as that of the more central parts of an organism ; and a similar persistence, becoming less and less detailed, extends outwards into the external environment. An organism and its environment are one, just as the parts and activities of the organism are one, in the sense that, though we can distinguish them, we cannot separate them unaltered, and consequently cannot understand or investigate one apart from the rest " (J. S. Haldane, *Organism and Environment, etc.* (1917), p. 98).

As with the species and the outstanding individual, so with the living parts of the organic whole. Every cell lives and moves in a living and commingling medium or environment of the total organism, the *milieu intérieur*. The life of the cell is a metabolism—a living taking from its living and homogeneous environment, a transforming appropriation, and a rendering or reproduction in return—with a breaking down and casting off of that which is exhausted. Each cell shares in the metabolic activity of the whole organism. Together they form a community of life. The behaviour of each is dependent on the behaviour of the rest ; and the lives of all are mutually regulated by each other.

Thus metabolism is the keynote of cell-life. One is tempted to apply the word metaphorically to the inter-relations and commingling of organism and environment. The organism absorbs, transforms, and excretes parts of its environment ; and what it throws off is absorbed and transformed by the environment in turn. Strict mutuality may be lacking, since the environment can scarcely be regarded as organic or in all respects alive ; and often, apparently without imparting of its substance, it affects the organism.

The universal business of all organisms is to get food and propagate their species. Their food and their own organic means of getting and assimilating it may be the main factor in the evolution of the myriad species of organisms with their varied faculties, from the grass of the fields to the elephants who devour it, and even man.

Still more broadly speaking, the sustaining, conditioning, permeating environment, and the reactions of the organism upon it, control the evolution of all organisms. Every organism fits its environment; and the evolution of species in the past must have held to the grooves of a like fitness, which are channels of possibility. Assuredly, as we find them, fishes cannot breathe in the air, nor land-animals beneath the water. The musk-ox and the polar bear seem to have developed their shaggy coats to meet arctic inclemencies, and would die if suddenly transferred to the equator. Such growths or evolutions, which are supposed to have gone on through uncounted millenniums, are understood inferentially. But that the coercions and opportunities of their environment, while obtaining food and shelter and keeping themselves from being eaten, mould the habits and develop the faculties of every animal, is a daily fact patent to any observer.

Of this coercive development, man, the human animal, was to afford complex illustration in the economic laws which spring in the first instance from his physical environment. Doubtless the means by which men obtain life's necessities go far to shape their institutions and the forms of their social development, as we may note hereafter. Neither the necessities nor the means of satisfying

them are stationary; but together expand and
multiply with the advance of society. From the
hunting of savages for food and skins, on through
more settled agricultural stages, to the furthest and
most complicated states of industrialism, such as
we labour under to-day—throughout this whole
social advance the expanding physical needs of
men, and the methods used to satisfy them, do not
cease to affect the development of social laws and
political institutions. Expanding needs work upon
society in correspondence with the machinery and
means through which these needs are satisfied.
Industrial progress moulds itself to the conditions
of environment. Advance is made along the lines
of the preponderance of impulse or compulsion,
which may operate through the pressure of class
on class, or evince itself in riots, industrial strikes,
and the application of police or military force.

Through this kind of progress or arrest, the logic
of fact, the possibilities of a situation, shake out
into some coherent, demonstrative result. Social
and political theorizing may help to clarify men's
minds, may exert influence, or contribute to explosions; but, whether through explosions or less
violent action, they will prove constructive only
when agreeing with the faculties and dispositions
of men and the possibilities of their environment.

This power of fact, this necessity of the actual
situation, works onward, altering social relations,
building cohesive human institutions and destroy-

ing them ; thus working constant change, and itself changing with changing conditions which it has done so much to bring about. Individual genius assists by suggesting outlets and escapements, improved mechanical devices, or a better adjustment of human relations, making for social peace and welfare.

III

Compulsions from Within

These constraints which seem to make their impact upon man from without, are linked to the compulsions arising from the physical nature of man, and from his disposition, his inherited, possibly cell-born character. The *genus homo* is thought to have attained human form through the working of the same factors which promoted the evolution of lower or prior organisms.

But perhaps in the case of man their relative importance may have changed. It is not maintained that evolution takes place, or has taken place, at the same rate, or at any constant rate, with all plants and animals. Certain kinds of ants, for example, appear to have remained static for millions of years. Apparently the evolution of species is no more universal or invariable throughout the organic world than progress is among the races of mankind. Some human races have never, to our knowledge, made discernible progress, whatever may have been their course before they swam into our historic ken. There have been times of retrogression even with progressive peoples. The so-called civilized world threatens to retrograde to-day. So we seem entitled to suppose that in the presumptive evolution of *genus homo*, the intelligence and social instincts of this animal may have played a larger rôle than with other animal forms. But of this intelligence hereafter.

Turning from the species to the individual, the opinion is that the determinants of individual growth lie inscrutably and implicitly in the egg and in the sperm, the germ-cells of the mature individual.[1] As the mollusc or the starfish, so the adult ape, or the human individual, lies implicit in its germ cells. Upon their conjunction, to wit, upon the fertilization of the egg, the man or woman is started on a career of individual growth and action which never shall shake loose from the inherent or inherited qualities of the original germinating cells—the true birth cells. And behind those birth cells, what hundred-handed animality, what hosts of bestial ancestors—likewise in the egg. And all endowed with life and impulse !

The race is in the individual, and the individual may sum up the race and be enchained by it. Nay, the individual is still part of the ancestral cave, the

[1] As to their infinite and living complexity, see Edmund B. Wilson, *The Physical Basis of Life* (The Yale Press, 1923).

many ancestral caves, from which the race has issued.[1]

But an individual is biologically a community. Its life, its physiology, is made up of the functioning, one might almost say, the lives, of organic parts. Among these there is co-ordination ; they constitute a living order of mutual enablement and regulation, and even competition.

This association of organic parts, this individual, makes one of a larger society of organisms or individuals like himself. The functional co-ordination within him is the biological analogue to his membership in this larger order. His social instincts and sense of kind press to an outward manifestation reflecting his physiological constitution. In himself the individual is a symbol of the social state.

Accordingly, like the lives of the parts within him, the individual's life shows two closely related sides. Each part within, each cell, takes its sustenance from its cognate and homogeneous environment, while at the same time contributing to the co-ordinated life of the whole organism, in which it lives and moves and has its being, severed from which it quickly dies. So the life of the whole organism, that is, the individual, appears twofold. He gets his food as he may, even through violence

---

[1] " In a living organism the past lives on in the present, and the stored adaptations of the race live on from generation to generation, waking up into response when the appropriate stimulus comes, just as conscious memory is awakened " (J. S. Haldane, *o.c.* p. 98).

to others ; and will fight fiercely for the chance to propagate. But his instinct of kind and his, or rather *her*, passion of parenthood, draw this him or her toward their like, and lead them to co-operate with their kin in mutual aid and protection. Sometimes, indeed, the dependence of individuals upon the rest of the community may almost approach the dependence of a body-cell. Many species of ants and bees are so elaborately organized in mutual dependence and for mutual aid and supplementing of function, that they could not sustain themselves as solitaries ; and the whole community, according to the equipment of its several divisions, is devoted to the care and protection of the young.[1]

Throughout the animal kingdom, including man, we may follow these varied aspects of the individual's apparently twofold life. But this life in reality is not dual, but one. It is a manifestation of that which can exist and live only as united in co-ordination. Every animal is a whole and entire organism. His or her life is not two but one throughout all its varied impulses, needs, and actions. He or she presses for food ; sex is vibrant and seeks its satisfaction. Parenthood and its devotions are another manifestation of this life ; and the broader communal instincts move toward

[1] Cf. W. M. Wheeler, *Ants, their Structure, etc.*, and his Lowell Lectures on " The Social Life of Insects," printed in the *Scientific Monthly* in June 1922 and following numbers. Also Prince Kropotkin, *Mutual Aid, a Factor in Evolution* (London, 1910).

its fulfilment.   They also are in and of this individual
life, germane to it, and make for its enrichment as
well as for its protection.

The constituents of the human animal are infinite.
Myriad are the factors entering his life, striking
upon it, moulding it, limiting and conditioning, and
again becoming very part of it.   They appear as
influences and compulsions from without, and as
determining inheritances, impulses, not to say
compulsions, from within.

Thought of in terms of evolution, fathomless
depths of elemental potencies and animal impulse
lie behind and within the animal nature of man.
The instincts of the animal kingdom are our instincts
and move our social life.   We seem to have had no
hand in their making, any more than in the making
of the environment which enfolds, sustains, and
enters into us.

Yet out of these driven and determined impulses,
out of these animal instincts and perhaps animal
thoughts, obscure, suggested, and confused, the
qualities of the human mind apparently emerge,
and the intellectual powers of judgement and
selection.

IV

THE FREEDOM OF THE MIND

With this entrance on the contested province of
free intelligence and will, acting with conscious

repulsion, preference, and selection, we touch the
hem of distinctive human progress, and enter upon
our proper theme. Until the entry of this factor
of the free intelligence, whatever advance has taken
place in life has been but as the growth or evolution
of plant and animal organisms, which themselves
possibly have contributed to their development
through some dumb self-directing. But man's
endeavours to advance his life are more conscious
and articulate ; their essence lies in the articulate
consciousness of the attempt.

It is here, moreover, that we sense a seeming
antinomy, as we enter on the true human history
of mankind. We have been moving in the realm
of natural law, apparently determined in its conditions and its sequences. But now we seem to
touch a counter-principle of no-law, of choice,
rejection, or denial. And as we advance from the
obscurities of savagery, and its impelled existence, to
the doings of more civilized, historic humanity, this
counter-principle becomes more palpable and active.

The time - honoured question of human freedom
has, in the past, been chained to the wheels of
religious controversy. More recently it has become
interwoven with the changing questions and solutions of many-sided scientific inquiry. It involves
the constitution and significance of the universe,
at least so far as concerns us men.

Conceptions of growth, of development, of
evolution, of progress, dominate thought to-day.

Why not give these conceptions rein ? Doubtless the earth has undergone catastrophes enough ; and we still see cyclone and earthquake, and, in the world of man, tempestuous revolutions. Yet nature makes no leap. Events are led up to and finally occasioned by antecedents, themselves as regular in their course as in their consequences. Catastrophes do not occur uncaused. We could predict them if we knew enough. So we imagine ; and are even more certain that every living being is a process of growth and, next, of apparent disintegration and transformation into something else. Our convictions extend further—from individuals in their succeeding generations to the race or species, which likewise we conceive as a slower product of change and development, in fine, as an evolution. Whether or not these thoughts are doomed to future modification, they relate at present to every phase of energy and life, mechanical, chemical, biological, physiological, and psychological.

This being so, we are impelled to find subtly creative action within these processes of growth and evolution. Since life, as we know it, is possible only within conditions which the earth has not always afforded, there was a time when life was not. Therefore life must somehow through the aeons have become. Though an initial instant be inconceivable, nevertheless invisible beginnings, inscrutable becomings, lie behind the anatomies and the physiological functions of plants and animals.

Intangible are the origins of their somehow generated instincts; and subtle the commencement of the further and more distinctive mentality which seems to evince itself in the higher animals, and unmistakably in *homo sapiens*. Hence, our best present knowledge and analysis point to a practical creativeness throughout these universal processes of growth and evolution. Indeed fragmentarily glimpsed vistas of an infinite past disclose to us an evolution fulfilling the functions of divine creation. It may be all divine : life may be God immanent. Creation need not spring from a loud *fiat*, nor yet be catastrophic. It may proceed through inscrutable gradation.

Moreover, through evolution, just as well as through original or interposed creation, a series of organisms may change beyond direct recognition, and slough off all similitude to far-off ancestral antecedents. If this be true of the visible structure and physiology of plants and animals, why should it not hold in the evolution of instinct and mentality ? In either case, nature, or God, or evolution, makes no leap, yet reaches something as utterly different as if it had leapt.

Primitive instincts may change in the course of time, and show themselves in modes complex, advanced, and hardly recognizable. Somehow inscrutably, mentality begins to function in the higher animals, and manifests itself in man. The human mind develops; its range deepens and enlarges, gaining in richness and complexity. It evolves faculties of deliberation and choice. It becomes capable of freedom. Henceforth it must seek its goal in a more perfect intellectual and moral freedom.

Many are the arguments, and portentous is the logic, brought against human freedom. Yet freedom of choice, freedom of attention and volition, are of the essence of the discriminating mind. Arguments against free will make also against mind, against the valid existence and functioning of mind. If it be held that a free human will introduces a new force, disturbs the assumed constancy of energy in nature, the argument drives against the essential functioning of mind itself.

Herein mind seems to separate from matter and physical force. Assume that force as well as matter is constant in the universe. Has any one applied this principle convincingly to organic life growing in intricacy through the successive stages of the world? Apparently it is not true of mind and its manifestations. Look far back over the geologic record, and will it not appear that the amount of mental efficiency increased between the age of trilobites and the age of mammals? Does not the record of the latter age show that the stupider mammals preceded the cleverer ones, and disappeared before them? And was there not still more mind in *homo incipiens* and *homo sapiens* when he came?

So throughout articulate human history mental vigour seems to have increased, or to have waned occasionally. So far as may be observed, the sum total of mental energy, of knowledge or mental fact, of the apprehension and application of what is true for man, continually increases or diminishes. We note this not merely throughout history, but even more incontestably in ourselves and in our effect upon our fellows and theirs upon us. Exert your muscles, and force and heat are spent, and must be restored through food taken from without. And if you give a cupful of your blood, it is gone from you.

Not so if you give of your thought. Your thought, your own sum of knowledge, is not diminished, but may be added to in the imparting, as all teachers know. A man gives his intellectual, spiritual, moral self, and thereby augments the same, while increasing, as he may hope, like spiritual elements in others. It is a spiritual rather than a physical law, that by giving himself a man gains and attains himself. The same is true of a society or people.

The results of biology seem not to be opposed to mental freedom; and no special argument of modern psychology is to be relied on against our conviction of the same based on our consciousness and extended experience. The history of every science, in disclosing the fallibility of our apprehension of any series of facts and the insufficiency of our data for broad assured conclusions, justifies us in hesitating to anchor our vital convictions to any single line of scientific argument. Look into the tangle of the mind as disclosed to modern analysis, examine its conscious thinking, its unconscious trains and potencies, and then decide whether any one factor in human opinion is solely to be relied on amid this interplay or entanglement of human whims and wishes and aberrations, and possibly with an unanalysable mental person somewhere behind them all. It is the mind itself, desirous to know more and understand, which the new psychologies of stimuli and reflexes do not explain. The search for knowledge cannot be put in terms of mechanics, or chemistry, or tropisms. All such may help us to understand the pit from which we have been digged, and by God's grace have striven to dig ourselves. But they do not reach the heights on which we try to stand, nor our sublime aspirations—themselves not utterly void of guidance for our convictions and our conduct.

Alas ! the freedom of the mind is a problem large and vague ; the horns of its dilemmas enclose the universe. Though usually conscious of our freedom, our convictions may waver with our arguments. If as physicists or chemists, or perhaps as biologists, we draw near the question through the course and routine of physical antecedent and consequent, it is difficult to escape from the determined sequence, or find place for the undetermined action of volition.

It is but natural that this approach through physics should lead to a conclusion of complete determinism, since it does not include the one factor in which freedom is most likely to be found, the human mind. Nor does it take full account of organic, though unthinking life, which shows whims of its own, and is not yet wholly predictable. If we regard the action of our own minds, or consider the conduct and achievements of the great men of history, we shall not abide by any such conclusion. Perhaps we shall find the human mind acting in freedom, even under the will of God.

Now since we are historians and humanists, and but casual amateurs of physics, our convictions are likely to be on the side of freedom. Only looking backward we recognize, in the spirit of our age, that the freedom of the human mind did not break forth with suddenness. Behind it lies admittedly the more automatic life of beasts and plants, the controlling qualities of the human germ-cells, and the mysterious pre-natal life of every human individual. Infused with masterful and plastic life, the human embryo makes its manifold and marvellous advance from the fertilized egg to the fully formed human being that emerges from the womb. One would not ascribe judgement and will to the embryo, nor much to babyhood. But something like judgement and free determination comes with the growth of body and mind and the impress of experience through the years of childhood and youth. With the better individuals, the same declares itself through the coming years with ever clearer consciousness and purpose.

The data upon which the mind may act are given by man's inheritance and environment. Its action corresponds with the character and the entire instinctive and mental nature of the individual. Many of the problems are set, and the solutions suggested, if not compelled ; yet complete slavery to suggestion and solicitation has not been demonstrated to our satisfaction. There is a residuum of freedom. While conceivably this might narrow down to a selection of alternatives, usually the conflicting dynamics of human nature do not adjust themselves to a simple " either—or," and human conduct is apt to flutter. Nevertheless, the wilful choices of the mind are the true human factors in human progress or retrogression. And sometimes these decisions of the free intelligence show themselves so apparently adverse to the leading of circumstance and material advantage, so disregardful of it all, as to make a true antinomy, a conflicting principle of will athwart the sequences of natural law.

Through the course of recorded history, the free will of the human mind, the whim, the arbitrary resolve or refusal, are seen to play their parts. The records may be superficial, or may speak with profound truth. The heroes of history are fettered by necessity, and yet are free. And each one of us recognizes in himself or herself the tried validity of this view. We realize our compulsions and our limitations; often feeling that we have done just what we had to, or have accomplished all that was within us to achieve. Yet we are conscious of our freedom—each of us the mirror of mankind, bound and free.

A certain flinging free from the age-long operation of natural law is suggested by the extraordinary social, economic, and intellectual progress of mankind within that brief space of time covered by articulate history. Groping backwards through the buried vestiges of the human or semi-human record, the evolution of man seems slow and geologic. But as the story emerges into the twilight of historic times, apparently the human development quickens, moving forward with the acceleration of a long led up to culmination. Some races indeed seem to remain as unprogressive as birds and beasts. But with other more favoured or gifted peoples it is as if new factors of progress had come into play.

Practically this is true. Human beings had reached such degree of mastery over the surrounding savagery of nature, that the advancing minds of men could more freely exercise discrimination. The human mind was coming to its own, and flinging itself forward along the path of ever more efficient freedom. The slow processes of nature—natural selection, mutation, what you will—were now to be outstripped by human energies working at last with a leaven of judgement, freedom, and spiritual impulse.

V

THE CRITERION OF THE WHOLE MAN

Not only human freedom, but the providence and very existence of God are contested—as they have been before, and many times. Yet we will still maintain both God and human freedom. Mankind is as a meteor in the vast expanse of slow creation. What do we know of any why and whence and whither ? Nevertheless, under the human (not bestial) impulse to know and understand, we press and are pressed onward. In our search for further and further knowledge, it is for us to employ all the data and all the means of ascertainment and suggestion within our reach. Who would think of rejecting physical science—the direct observation of nature and its operations, the investigation of force and life, of the whole range of inanimate and animate phenomena ? Who would reject this method, prosecuted in modern times with such glorious energy and success ? But the advance of youthful and lusty science leads on to constant surprise, if not reversal. There seems no end to Nature's surprises, no bottom to her mysteries.

We are still profoundly justified in holding our intellectual judgement in suspense. Science has its inning, and we wish it Godspeed. But there may be other vessels of the Lord, other ways of truth. Time and again men have set themselves to win certitude of knowledge through following the dialectic of their own intellectual processes into the ultimate reaches of metaphysics. They were forced to this by the contradictions of their immediate perceptions of themselves and the world about them. Often through intending the mind on its own processes and shortcomings, they have risen to schemes of things covering the universe and touching the ultimate realities. But the certitudes reached by paths of metaphysics have been shaken, and after many centuries different-minded men began to find all such conclusions vain and such controversies futile. The direct investigators of nature scorned metaphysics, not realizing that aforetime the crude physical hypotheses of the early Greeks had called forth those schemes of thought which were designed to obviate sense contradictions. Even to-day physical science is constantly lured beyond its depth to metaphysics, as we shall note hereafter.

Yet, no man of science would wish to cast himself again into those dark gulfs. And we who have not given our lives to physical science, but as historians may profess to some acquaintance with the follies of mankind and the blind alleys of thought, no more than the scientists would we again trust our intellectual fortunes exclusively to the labyrinths of our inner consciousness or to the sole pointings of

our furthest aspirations. We, too, will be taught of
all that science has to teach us, for the betterment of our lives and the enlargement of our
wisdom. Nor will we discard those larger reasonings, possibly more profound and apparently less
secure than the inferences of physical science, which
we set under the name of philosophy and even dub
metaphysics.

Nevertheless, for the larger judgements and
decisions of life, the final criterion of truth and
value lies in the total sum of our experience. Regard
must be had to the totality, if not the wholeness, of
our natures, in which our faculties are bound
together, and either co-operate or act as checks
upon each other. The different faculties subtly or
palpably affect each other's behaviour, or combine
or dovetail in their contribution to human actions
and reactions. Each faculty has a validity of its
own, and may claim to count in the estimate of
human welfare, and in the determination of what
is true, as well as what is right, for man.[1]

It may be, for example, that *wish*, the quality of
desire, is never absent from our thinking, and that
it influences the profoundest, the most abstract or
detached conceptions of our minds. Possibly all
our mental acts are of the whole self, or at least of

---

[1] There is biological analogy or argument for this view.
No single part or organ is supreme in the animal organism,
or can perform its office except as a part or function of the
whole.

the whole of that one of our changing selves which is operative at the moment. Thinking carries a conative and emotional quality, if only less markedly than it involves the energies of what seems sheer intellection—the action of what we call the perceptive and reasoning faculties. Indeed, an ideal, an attempt to conceive what is most desirable, and perhaps a volition to attain it, is involved in the best and most strenuous human thinking—as with Plato, for example. Assuredly wish, and even passion, are never utterly absent from the highest human thought.

It is when our professedly detached reason seeks to set itself apart from the human whole, that it most reasonably may be mistrusted. Yet still more, on the other hand, should men beware of their palpably emotional or passionate impulses, or even aspirations, when these energize without the control or guidance of the judgement which arises from reflection—reflection seeking to embrace every consideration offered by all the knowledge humanly available for the decision trembling on the lips or touching the act for which the body throbs. The action of impulse or passion, without the foreseeing eye of judgement, is only too likely to make for destruction and human bestiality.

One need not find that all human truth is held in rational knowledge; and one may well guard against pedantic and dialectic rationalism, the shrivelled fruit of case-hardened methods of think-

ing in fixed logical categories that have become
inelastic, unfluid, static, incapable of adaptation to
the realities of any and all sorts of experience
impressing human consciousness. Why need the
intellect hold aloof from other ways of knowing
and judging ? Let it be still the guide and pilot,
or at least the final judge of what the other faculties
have done and of their novel apperceptions. But
let the court have all the data, look every witness
in the face, and be not over-ready to declare one or
another unworthy of belief on oath, or his testimony
irrelevant, impertinent, and inadmissible. Then
there need be no question of the propriety and great
importance of maintaining the ultimate authority
of such a court of reason, nor need appeal be taken
to ignorant emotion and a sentimentality which
will not be instructed.

Yet so long as there are depths in our natures
which the intellect has not plumbed, and shady
places where no light of science has penetrated, we
are justified in looking to our natures in their
wholeness, and to those human or divine hopes and
aspirations which, through the long panorama of
history, by thorny and uneven paths seem to have
led on and upward. These we will still include
within the data of our judgements upon life.

VI

The Hypothesis of God in Human History

Men's best hopes and aspirations have paralleled their conceptions of the Divine. Men have striven as they have conceived God to have led them. And still for a conception of the universe the hypothesis of God is better than any no-hypothesis of no-God. The thought of God arises from the convergence of our intellectual needs and noblest human impulses. We may not throw aside our furthest spiritual insistences.

One feels convinced of God: how shall we conceive and think Him, so as to justify our surrender to His influence, or to the impulse of our passionate conviction?

First, in relation to natural or physical law. The whole natural world and the sidereal universe, so far as known, follow regular sequences, bound by the laws or nature of their substances, energies, and relations. Physical law is of the essence of inorganic matter or energy. It also enters and to a vast extent controls organic life, determining the forms and functioning of plants and animals, and apparently even the scintillae of mentality discerned in animals below the state of man. Their volitional or mental freedom is doubtful; their instincts and impulses or quasi-thoughts seem but expressions of their physical organisms, though perhaps suggesting something more. Natural law likewise determines not merely the bodily functions, but the bulkier portion of the impulses and perceptions of mankind.

The sequences which we group under the general concept of natural law seem to belong to matter or to physical energy.[1] The relation of Something or Some One, *i.e.* God, to matter or physical energy or law, seems a problem of creation, or of the contribution of energy or the bestowal of life or evolutionary power. It is a superhuman problem, and any conceivable solution is altogether beyond our knowledge or experience, and perhaps beyond our powers of thought. Nor is it a problem of practical moment for mankind. Because just as natural law works in apparently unswerving sequences, so, in respect to these sequences, God is equally obdurate and ineluctable, or, perhaps, hardly conceivable as free. Vainly will man lift his hands to God to stay the earthquake or the tempest or bring rain upon the earth ; or to stop the ravening of jungle beasts or invisible germs whose homing or multiplying means the sickness and death of men. We cannot stay the sun, nor in the smallest material things prevent the course of natural law through prayer

[1] Linguistically *natura* is equivalent to φύσις, and the two words have a like range of meaning in Latin and Greek respectively. So natural law is equivalent to physical law. Yet " natural " has gradually acquired a broader or looser sense than " physical," and is not so definitely contrasted with " mental " or " spiritual."

to any God or gods. Yet we may profitably
remember that many philosophers and physicists,
from the earliest to the most recent times, have
seen in this unfailing operation of natural law the
profoundest evidence of a divine control.[1] Moreover, we may deem that the man whose prayers
cannot check the course of nature may still be
spiritually helped by them ; and it is very thinkable
that in answer to prayer God may turn physical ills
to the spiritual benefit of the responsive and faithful
sufferer.

So we turn to the God who is mind and love,
whether He be the same as the God of natural law
or quite another. Him we conceive to act with
that freedom of choice and discrimination which we
cannot dissociate from the functioning of mind.
We conceive God to act upon the minds and moods
of men as spirit addressing itself to spirit ; for men
are capable of being thus acted on, and moved and
drawn, perhaps to think and will as the Divine Spirit
thinks and wills. Freedom of mind is of the essence
of the action of God, and also of the essence of the
human response, acceptant or recalcitrant. Here
there is no coercion. The man is free to accept or
reject the grace of God.

Nevertheless, God's proffered inspiration or

[1] " Au vrai, il semble que rien ne manifeste ici-bas la
présence mystique du divin autant que cette harmonie éter-
nelle et inflexible qui lie les phénomènes et qu'expriment les
lois scientifiques " (C. Nordmann, *Einstein et l'univers* (Paris,
Hachette, 1921), p. 190). (Eng. Trans. by M'Cabe, p. 207.)

guidance and man's acceptance or rejection, although free, are not exempted from the law of consequences. Inevitably the human spirit is raised or lowered by its acceptance or refusal, as in its heightened or blunted power of further response.

The cruder religions have more to do with the needs and cravings of men's bodies than with the aspirations of their minds. The primitive God divides the Red Sea or feeds His people with manna in the wilderness, or, as Indra or Zeus, may wield the thunderbolt. The gods send shipwreck or plagues. The arrows of Apollo smite men with mortal bodily disease. Such gods are very powerful, but are not philosophically conceived as infinite or omnipotent.

With advancing thought religions become more spiritual,[1] and the intercourse between the higher type of worshipper and his god may relate itself more genially to the condition and action of the spirit—the spirit or impassioned mind of man seeks the aid of God to save or purify or ennoble it. Yet in all ages the vast majority of men have been concerned with material welfare, and only the finer sort with the interests of the soul or mind. This

---

[1] The Jewish religion tended to become spiritual through the generations of the prophets, till it may be said (loosely speaking) to have culminated in Jesus and Paul. But as common beliefs are always below the spirituality of religious leaders, so the subsequent general acceptance and interpretation of the gospel of a supreme Founder falls in an indefinite number of ways from its high pattern.

D

is still true, while it is more true than ever that the religion, the faith, of the " finer sort " relates to the needs and aspirations of the mind or yearning spirit. Our God is God of our mind and spirit; it is to our minds that He speaks, and our minds that He persuades or inspires to His purposes. We come close to Him—for is He not within our minds ? —in prayer for wisdom and righteousness, and not in foolish petitions touching our bodies or the material things of living on the earth. In the spirit He is our God, and we are His spiritual children communing with Him in the spirit.[1]

As for the part this God of ours has taken in the world-drama, whether or not He built the stage and made the actors out of nothing, we believe that He is furthering the *dénouement* and climax of the play. We look back over the record of life upon this earth, and we perceive life inscrutably beginning, persisting, and advancing into more complex and agile and subtle forms : life, as it were, inclusive, the life of plants and beasts and men, of the marvel-

[1] Thus we rely upon the immediacy of our religious experience—which is spiritual. But the crasser, earlier man, or, indeed, the crasser present man and woman, may have had, and may still have, an immediacy of religious experience arising from things physical and relating to them, having to do with the crashing powers of nature, or with physical disease. And so men still pray for many kinds of things. Religious men cannot help praying for whatever they want very much, whether or no their minds bid them to expect it in answer to prayer. It is the chief mode of their communion with the Great Companion.

lously living bodies of the same, and of the progressing mentalities of those that have minds. Such progress goes on, even through destruction, mutual preying of its agents upon each other, and through the blind rapine of mankind. It goes on more genially through the growth of social impulses and the devotion of human beings to others. We conceive that God is the benevolent, and perhaps struggling, spirit of this progress, even its enabling power, and the Conceiver of the plan. Throughout history He has been aided by "His servants the prophets," by His loving children, and by those also who are touched by His fire, though they may know Him not, while they strive to extend knowledge and wisdom on the earth—which is God's truth and wisdom and knowledge.

May we not even think that the expanding consciousness of the human race, from its bestial beginnings, has in some way reflected the consciousness of God ? If so, is there not progress in God Himself, in the Divine Spirit, as well as in man ? And if God is reflected in the spiritual consciousness of the human race, is He not then Himself conceivably a spiritual growth, development, or evolution ?

Such thoughts of God the Spirit need not commit us to any logical conclusion in a metaphysical dualism. Rather, we register a *non intelligo* as to the origins of the physical universe and the laws of matter. But as for God the Spirit, we may call Him the Good Spirit, inasmuch as most of the pain and evil in the world—even spiritual evil—seems to flow from the pull of matter and its ways upon our minds. Spiritual goodness may be less impeded as it becomes freer—that is, as it frees itself from the drag and push of matter. We may conceive our God as righteous in His nature, and through the very working of His nature making for good.

In imagining or in justifying our ideas of a living, working God who is Spirit, one need not struggle for an impossible consistency. Our conviction registers our most catholic response to all of life and its myriad facets of suggestion. Too many diverse and indeed contrary reflections enter this our convinced scheme of the divine life and function ; it will not lack many a logical contradiction, being itself composed of feelings and intuitions as well as of some rational considerations.

But in our inconsistency we keep great company ! No working religion ever has been consistent in the idea of its God. Indeed, the endeavour for such consistency means scholasticism. The religion that is living, like life itself, knows no consistency, which is of logic. Through Greek literature, the thought of Zeus is constantly running through all the compass of the notes, from vengefulness and lust to moral sublimity. In the Old Testament, Jehovah presents more phases of tribal or cruel, or again of universal, deity than he has canonical interpreters.

And in the Gospels, he who would make a logical consistency of God the Father and His Son must sift the utterances shrewdly ! Through the coming ages the working faith of Christians was not to be handicapped with any logical consistency. Not through logic is religion justified of her children.

Obviously, then, with our present convictions as to human growth and evolution, and our tolerant historical interpretations, we need no longer stumble at the crude or harsh conceptions of the Divine obtaining among past men ; nor, on the other hand, need we be troubled by the dogmatic and ultimate conclusions of metaphysical theologians which do not seem to tally with the phenomena of life. We have the same right to our own ideas, which it is our duty to enlarge and raise to the limits of our thinking and desires, and keep in accord with our vital convictions.

The elements of the discussion are endless, and one may not always argue fruitfully with our friends of different tempers and equal or greater intelligence, who can always show a *con* for any of our *pros*. It may be a question of temperament ; but, as in one's own life one may gratefully recognize divine promptings and the leading care of God, so one may find in history the impulse of divine inspiration, as well as a universal plan and a divine standard and providence. I cannot regard the human story, and the whole unending growth and sloughing off of thought and temper, as a driven sequence of generat-

ing conditions and unavoidable result. I cannot
think it so simply or so brutally. It is complex
beyond any likely reach of our analysis. And it
seems to me not altogether reducible to the palpable
and quantitative; for it is impressed with a certain
human unaccountability. It seems permeated with
arbitrary freedom; and its regularity or certainty
of sequence is impinged upon and often foiled by
the aberrations of human whim, if not by some
incomprehensible power. I do not altogether understand history; I cannot explain much that has
taken place. And I feel it safer to assume the
constant or occasional participation of unfathomable
elements—the animating and inspiring providence
of God, the potent waywardness of human genius.
The whole seems to me no brutally necessitated
process into which all of us are drawn as helpless
atoms, but in which the free dignity of man should
decline to take futile part. It still seems to me
that each thinking pigmy of us need feel no shame
to play his small incalculable rôle, nor fear to do
so, knowing well that no child's hand shall much
derange the world.

VII

PROGRESS TOWARD FREEDOM

Yet we would not fail to recognize the unceasing
and age-long working of physical or natural law in
the evolution or creation of man, and its indelible

effect upon his entire organism and social progress. The needs of the body did not cease to constrain mankind through all stages of social and political development. So through all the historic periods we must accept not only the operation of natural law, but the continuing effect of animal impulse, which impregnates human nature through its long inheritance, and still measurably shapes the conduct of men and women. All these compulsions act as the vibrant and energizing background of human life.

It is from these basic assumptions and admissions that we rise to a consideration of the progress of human endeavour, which with some conscious impulse for betterment advances through increasing knowledge and clearer discrimination. Whatever may be the ultimate grounds of this progress, it has been the immediate achievement of the human mind working (with the aid, as we believe, of God) through increasing knowledge, for the attainment of an ampler and nobler, more spiritual and lasting, well-being. It is all a progress toward a more complete and inclusive freedom. Its furthest reaches will be won through the enfranchised power of the mind intent upon its various aims with conscious purpose; an intending of the mind which is, or may be called, the will resolved through the free action of the intelligence.

The early impulse toward knowledge relates itself to a conception of the consequences of conduct, and to the law or power by which they are brought about. The desire to know was utilitarian in motive, and even while man was scarcely man it addressed itself to the threatening or favourable aspects of his environment, and to what might follow upon his acts.

But although occupied with immediate needs, the human mind at as early a period as we have knowledge of is found set upon the endeavour to reach some sort of scheme of things, crudely intelligible and at the same time moral and religious. The last words imply that this intelligible scheme must embrace man's relationship to the objects and powers about him, malign or benevolent. In all of this the mind not only seeks consistency or unity, but has always, as it were, started from unity, looked out upon its quest from the oneness of its own organic personality. In archaic times thought had made no spectrum analysis, had seen no clear distinction between those many sides of human perplexity which severally should issue in religion, in philosophy, and in physical science. But all these matters lay implicit, entangled, and unresolved within man's early endeavour to imagine or conceive the nature and dynamics of the powers about him and his adjustment with their action.

As human thought progresses it becomes more analytical; it will distinguish between the many provinces of its activities. Yet, since they continue to issue from the unit man, and from the inter-

relation of his interests, the compass of his thought
and desire will never lose its vital unity of relationship to the desirous thinker. All branches of
human thought, all strainings of the human spirit
and the lusts and cravings of the flesh can never
spring utterly apart and proceed in separate isolation without loss of the life inherent in their catholic
sonship to their human source. Every moral,
religious, or intellectual interest must keep its ties
of home.

The contribution of each people or exceptional
individual to the conception of this scheme of things
was scarcely in the nature of exact truth, whatever
that may be. Yet humanity's intellectual advance
was somehow aided and the human capacity for
spiritual freedom increased. Thoughts might be
lost, temporarily or for ever; but each had added
something, or effected something, even though the
effect seemed confined to the thinker's mind.
Indeed, thoughts, though submerged, are more
rarely lost, and are apt to re-emerge, at least in
their effects. The more dynamic thoughts worked
themselves into the spiritual life of races, moving
them onward. To-day we are the heirs of all the
ages, and who shall say what conceptions from the
past are not somehow, consciously or subconsciously,
held in our own thoughts and temperaments?
They are not all truths for us; they may be contra-
dictory; yet they still have strength for guidance
or repulsion. Humanity's lines of spiritual progress,

broken though they be, point somewhither —
possibly to the truth of God to which we are ever
seeking to draw near.   They point along the waver-
ing parallels of humanity's endeavour to become
more like the Good, the Wise, the Divine, however
we would phrase it.   They point true, to the best
truth for men, whatever may lie beyond our present
ken or beyond the grave.

From this survey of the course of man's emergence
from the brute we turn to examples of human
progress.

CHAPTER II

I

PRIMITIVE STAGES

ALL manner of physical coercions and opportunities affect the human race emerging from the brute. " Catch as catch can " applies to the development of faculty and habit not merely with lions, antelopes, and monkeys, but with men. The parental and communal or group instincts, which maintain the tribes of animals, are also manifested in mankind. Human beings have always nurtured, protected, and helped each other, have fought for one another as well as for themselves.

Thought combines with instinct to produce habits and customs, which become institutions. Both the self - assertive and the self - sacrificing sides of human life—the twofold life which still is one [1]— enter into the shaping of the family, the group, the

---

[1] *Ante*, p. 13 *sqq.*

tribe, the state, in fine, into the development of social and political, as well as religious, institutions. The balance and adjustment of these two sides of human life constitute the law and justice of a community or state.

This age-long story is a myriad-sided one. For it is the story of the interplay, or tragic inter-working, of human faculty, of human nature and its growing knowledge, and the equally complex facts of the human environment, the many different human environments. Its first chapter is the family, the primal human institution, which the human race adopted long before it was human. Man always was a family man! In the remote bestial past his and her sexual and parental instincts had evolved the family. Along with it, or perhaps afterwards in the case of the *genus homo*, the pack or herd, or group or tribe, comes into being, affording a larger safety and opportunity for mutual aid. Therewith arises necessary leadership, kingship eventually, and sometimes fighting bands, or groups of adult counsellors. Time will develop the social and political institutions of a complex civil community or state.

The earliest stages of family and social customs, and then of what may be called political institutions, show mankind but little freer than other animals. Like the ways of getting food, the other habits of the primitive family or group were largely determined by obvious exigency.

Very obscure is the temporal order of growth of early human institutions — of the family or the horde, of the custom of inheritance through the mother, through the father; of the origins of pastoral life, the beginnings of agriculture, the growth of councils, chieftaincies, and kings. Without adding to this already elaborate and largely inferential discussion, we may find enough difficulty in the question of the relative and proportionate effect on early social progress of the opportunities and coercions of environment, of the inwardly determined (rather than free) action of animal instincts, and of needs slowly becoming human, and, finally, of the entering influence of the more freely discriminating selective and devising mind.

Where *genus homo* first became *homo sapiens* is unknown. Perhaps the earliest advance toward what is called civilization was made in certain regions most favourable to assured human sustenance and comfort, to wit, Mesopotamia and the valley of the Nile. The fertile soil was the gift of a river; and one might be tempted to call the Mesopotamian and Egyptian civilizations river gifts, did we not realize that a prosperous and stable society, with its component laws and customs and observances as well as its material goods, can never be the simple gift of any soil and climate, however beneficent, but must also be the fruit of human faculties working under these favourable conditions.

A partially free human industry and ingenuity must have taken part.[1]

Soil, climate, physical conditions generally, will direct the manner in which primitive men must get their food—whether it be by fishing, for example, or by caring for flocks, or cultivating the soil. Fertility of soil, regularity of climate and supply of moisture facilitate agriculture, and with its sure rewards impel men to labour. A hot or cold climate will determine the nature of the requisite tenting or housing; and such clay as Mesopotamia afforded leads men to build with brick, as forests suggest the use of wood. Yet in no case can we conceive the method of working the soil or using materials for building as completely determined or entirely accidental. Nature affords materials,

---

[1] There is validity in the so-called "economic view of history," so long as economic considerations are not made the whole story, or given the leading part. No open-minded historian could accept the extreme statements of Marx, made in the introduction to his *Criticism of Political Economy*.

I should not be willing even to put the matter as strongly as in the following statement from p. 67 of E. R. A. Seligman's *Economic Interpretation of History* (N.Y., 1903) : "We understand, then, by the theory of economic interpretation of history, not that all history is to be explained in economic terms alone, but that the chief considerations in human progress are the social considerations, and that the important factor in social change is the economic factor. Economic interpretation of history means, not that the economic relations exert an exclusive influence, but that they exert a preponderant influence in shaping the progress of society." It seems to me that more weight should be given to self-esteem and the parental and group instincts and devotions.

sometimes in suggestive forms. She instructs by suggestion. But Nature did not make hooks or nets or snares and place them in men's hands with definite directions as to use; she did not quite make hoes or ploughs or shovels, nor such early primitive machines as the lever, the pulley, or the crank and axle, and the screw. Man made his tools or adapted them. From the rudest implement to the last devices of the modern motor, it was the devising ingenuity of man that fashioned and used the tool.

Perhaps there was less freedom in the motive than in the device. Men have always been impelled by need—of food, shelter, clothes—and by the instincts of sex, parentage, and kind. These desires are not free. Man is *driven* by them to use his wits. Need is the mother of invention. The Belly, as Rabelais says, is the mother of arts and sciences. Yet free (and not altogether determined) human ingenuity will always be at work even under the compulsion of these impulses.

Working thus to satisfy his needs, man is but half free. The end is implanted in him. But the further a human purpose separates itself from these unfree necessities, the more free it becomes. Apart from such compulsion, the mind may work with greater freedom. He alone is wholly free whose ends and purposes, as well as the means by which he seeks to accomplish them, spring from his freely discriminating and choosing mind. This is an ideal which no human being may quite achieve. Even in the freest, most self-directed life the cares of the body and common daily incidents bring the impact of a multitude of determining influences. Of course no human life is wholly free. Yet if we will approach the question along the ways of history, we shall see how some men have reached a large and genial, though imperfect, freedom. They may be free within the sphere of their deepest purposes.

So men were never utterly bound by the conditions of their environment. Choice creeps in. There is some scanted freedom even in the filling of primitive needs. Through inventions and improvements men become less driven; and upon the satisfaction of their peremptory needs comes greater opportunity for self-direction. A partial self-direction proceeds along the path of obtaining more of the material goods of life than their simple or driven needs had called for. To amass wealth and all material objects of desire may become an aim, suggested, indeed, and yet continued with a decision or choice, which selects it as the best thing in life. Men still incline to this aim. The ancient Phoenicians, venturesome, persistent, and ingenious, seem to have been possessed by it.

A more ancient race (if indeed there be a difference in the age of races) developed a vaster civilization in the Nile valley. A king, or Pharaoh, had grown to monstrous proportions. It may be that the character and contour of that narrow strip of river land, entirely dependent for its fertility upon the inundation of the Nile, operated to deliver absolute power into the hands of him who could control the distribution of the waters. At all events, the people had become servile, and the Pharaohs and great nobles compelled them under the sticks of task-masters to build their pyramids and palaces and temples. The rule of the Pharaohs did not altogether lack beneficence. Egypt's prodigious monuments still astound us ; and the Egyptian civilization was fertile in devices to make life comfortable and adorn it with things of art and beauty. Yet the mind of the people remained servile, bound by long acquiescence in the right of others to dominate them, control their labour, and use it for ends carrying small benefit to the labourer. Chained by such acceptances, the Egyptian mind possessed scant residue of freedom to take part in shaping Egyptian destinies.

The attainment of some degree of civic freedom among an aggregate of men large enough to con-stitute a people brings new interests and purposes. For this, the people, or rather individuals among them, must have the imagination to conceive and the boldness to demand more equable terms from their superiors. Such a mentality, with its con-tingent effect of social and political emancipation, enables men to choose an occupation, or task, or way of life, which possibly may lie outside the lines of the direct compulsion of their needs.

E

What we regard as civic freedom seems confined
to Europe, ancient and modern, and to our excess-
ively modern America, though in our own generation the contagion appears to have spread to Asia.
The past history of the vast peoples of China and
India illustrates different principles. China has
hitherto adhered to the Confucian scheme. A civic
order prescribed and administered authoritatively
from above has been the ideal for society and
government. Political freedom as conceived in
Europe has not been heard of. The individual has
pursued his progress within this frame of political
order, or disorder, regarding which he has had little
voice. Within this socially bounden life, as it seems
to us, the people, through their devout approval
and earnest observance, have fostered the Chinese
virtues of filial piety and of conformity to revered
rites and ceremonies, and have made them into a
willingly followed ideal. Within this fixed social
scheme individuals have developed tastes and
faculties for poetry and painting and for the crafts
which adorn dwellings and temples.

Perhaps the Confucian scheme itself, as we may
note hereafter, was China's chief contribution to
the store of human achievement. Quite otherwise
the great Indian contributions came from the
sublimated thinking of men whose aims were
detached from the frame and energizing of society.
What cared they for any civic freedom! The
liberty to direct their own lives freely amid the

affairs of society was but part of the dire net of life from which, through the exercise of a profounder spiritual freedom, they sought deliverance—as likewise we shall note.

II

THE EXAMPLE OF THE GREEK CITY-STATE

If Mesopotamia and the valley of the Nile fed men just for the turning of the soil, and if the heat and tumult of growth in India might move the contemplative mind to loathe the transitory, Greece, with her Asiatic coast, her islands and the penetrating sea, made an apt home for quick faculty and varied human trait. It was a land of harbours, surrounded and illumined by the sea ; a land to reward toil and yet not pamper ; a land of mountains and lovely valleys, with a variety of natural growths and yielding under cultivation grains and many kinds of fruits. By reason of isthmuses and mountain barricades small peoples could protect themselves. No part of Greece was naturally fitted to dominate the whole. The land favoured local independence, and might foster individual freedom in the members of that gifted race which were to make it their home.

A gifted race indeed ! That first clear testimony, the Homeric epics,[1] proves the Greeks gifted beyond

---

[1] The remains of the Cretan or Mycenaean civilization show the Greek race on the way to become itself distinctively.

other men, and shows them vibrant with the impulses and faculties of personal and civic freedom. The heroes are wonderfully and most novelly free.

The assembly of chiefs and people in the second book of the *Iliad* is perhaps our earliest record of the call and conduct of such a temperamental deliberative gathering. Having told his plan to a council of the chiefs, Agamemnon directs the heralds to call the host to an assembly. There he speaks with silly guile, proposing an abandonment of the hopeless war. As a natural though apparently unanticipated result, the people rise and rush for the ships. Odysseus is moved to stay their flight and press them to sit down again. Bandy-legged Thersites rises and reviles Agamemnon, and urges the host to return home and leave him to gather spoil and honours by himself—he who has dishonoured Achilles, a better man than himself. With this real grievance of the outrage put upon the best of the Greeks, Thersites insinuates his own valiant part in the war. Odysseus browbeats the demagogue and strikes him with his staff, and he sits down amid the rather tempered laughter of the rest. Then Odysseus, addressing Agamemnon, urges on the war; Nestor backs him, and Agamemnon, closing the harangues, gives orders for battle, with threats of death to those who skulk by the ships. The Argives shout aloud.

Doubtless the whole procedure is " heroic," and the host is expected to listen, not to argue. Nevertheless the call and meeting of the assembly, its changing mood and final tumultuous acceptance of the leaders' decision, assume some freedom of debate, though it behooves the speaker to be a man of worth.

The fall of Troy, Achilles' death, Odysseus' return, all were fated, with great propriety in accordance with inherent tendency or probability. But within this large web of fate, what freedom of whim and mood and action!—although death is fated for us all, yet while he lives man may be free. The Homeric thought of fate was a just judgement upon human life—free within the qualities of its nature and the bounds of its mortality.

Such conceptions of freedom within bounds recognize the law of consequences, that when the doer has done a wicked fatal act, the act and its entailments become as fate to the doer, who must expiate. So in Aeschylus and Sophocles Fate becomes ethical; but the doer in his initial act is free.

As the Greeks balanced fate and freedom, so in their judgement of human lots, of human happiness and misfortune, their judgement did not wince. Their natures were eager, their desires intense; fulfilment brought joy. Yet human fortunes were overshadowed by mortality, and often overthrown at the outset or in mid-course. There was ill in every life, and in some lives some good. So they judged fairly, not cursing or rejecting life nor thoughtlessly Utopian.

Thoughtfulness in conduct, the habit of thinking before acting, was a trait ascribed by Pericles to his Athenians, and he might have included other Greeks. But thoughtfulness in conduct is of the essence of freedom, or may be, when the man is not over-thoughtful and despondent. Greeks loved action as well as consideration.

In the routine of life which human beings lead or are pushed along by needs and instincts, gaining livelihood or wealth, and caring for wives and children, Greeks were as free as might be—that is, partially free in their ingenuity and device of means, though the motive was a natural need. It was in the use of wealth when gained, and of the leisure which it brought, that the Greeks reached more complete freedom. Here came freedom in the choice of life and the thought of its object.

We may still take the Athenians as our best example, since they seem as the crown of all the Greeks, and also have told us more about themselves. Greek civilization, and, above all, the Athenian, strikes us as urban, presenting examples of a completely corporate urban society ; for Greek society was closely inter-knit and corporate. But it was based on farming, and for the most part on the hard, precarious farming of small farm-owners. Agriculture is a form of labour never sneered at through all Greek literature.

The farmer worked to provide for his household. He did not expect wealth. He was a poor man essentially. And it is well to recognize that, like other Greeks, the Athenians in the early, as well as in the greatest, days of Athens were poor. They owned little ; their small unheated houses had few comforts ; their food might be scanty. There was always a dearth of accumulated wealth and credit for large enterprises. Only the city, at the time of her power and glory in the middle of the fifth century before Christ, had by the energy and devotion of her citizens, by her wars, her navy, and the tribute exacted from her allies for their defence, accumulated a large treasure. She was the mistress of the small sea-empire of the Aegean ; and she would use her treasure to embellish the city, strengthen the navy, and pay her own citizens for services performed with zeal and even with the complete sacrifice of their bodies and scanty fortunes.

The Athenian prized his freedom, the freedom of his mind and will to apply the energies of mind and body to whatever purpose or occupation should be judged best. His ends assuredly embraced his own well-being, and just as assuredly, in the great days of Athenian citizenship, embraced the well-being of his city, without which his own life was but as wreckage from a shattered ship.

His nature vibrated with energy. He was not lazy, but disliked drudgery, which he would undergo only under the compulsion of need or some important end. His sense of human well-being sought to be quit of the daily drudgery involved in human needs. If the women and slaves worked for him, he would have more time and energy to devote to the noble or interesting things of life. He could take part in politics, be a magistrate perhaps, or listen as a juryman to the trial of exciting causes, and help to decide matters of moment for his city. He could be free to train his body for military or naval service, free to talk and listen in the agora or market-place, or devote his leisure to philosophy. The crafts were interesting; to be a stone-cutter, for example, and carve reliefs and statues or finish those marble drums that were going into the columns of the new temple to Athene. Such work gave opportunity for fashioning objects beautifully, as he and his friends loved to see them. But these drums were huge—what labour to cut them from the quarries of Pentelicus and then to drag them up to the Acropolis ; or what still worse and drearier labour was it to pick and hack the silver ore from the mines at Laureion, in the north-east of his peninsula ! How much better to have such drudging labour done by slaves, dull barbarians for the most part who had been bought or captured ! They were suited to it, or had to do it anyhow. Yet among them might be cleverer ones, too, fit to work in copper or make pottery, keep accounts, or attend to the booths about the market. They should be treated kindly, and the hope of freedom held before them to make them work more cheerfully. Many a slave was well treated and allowed to purchase his freedom in Athens, or given it by his master's testament.   So they became members of the numerous band of free residents who were not full citizens, but of mixed or foreign blood, Greek and barbarian. They, too, helped the community and enjoyed the privilege of living there, and earning wages, or selling their wares, or busying themselves in affairs. They served in the army, too, though rarely with the most honoured citizen soldiery of the heavy-armed.

So the Athenians through their own energies, and assisted by the labour of others, achieved an unexampled civic life and individual life as well. In the shaping of their laws and government, un-. doubtedly the promptings and quasi-compulsions of the human situation and the physical environment had great share; as always in the growth of institutions.   But it were peculiarly absurd to find Athenian institutions just the growth of a situation which they met or of the material needs they satisfied. Creative ingenuity had wrought in them, with an insistence on the people's part upon the free disposal of their surplus or super-energies. The freedom of the human mind never demonstrated itself in the shaping of human institutions more convincingly than in the Greek city-republics, and most wonderfully in Athens.

The Athenian scheme of government was animated with the assertion of human freedom. It lived and moved through insistence upon the right and duty of every citizen to share in the functions of the city—a city which offered each citizen opportunity for individual enterprise and development and held within its greater self the lives and fortunes of all. It was a scheme of government admirably illustrating the dual human impulse to fulfil the individual's life and help the community as well. The noted men who fashioned the Athenian constitution appear impelled with a purpose of inducing every citizen to take part in the common business of the city, and especially in the administration of justice among citizens, as a chief affair of all, pertaining to the essence as well as maintenance of civic freedom. The home policy, the democratic purpose of Solon, Cleisthenes, Pericles, kept in view an ever wider and more attractive distribution of civic duties and responsibilities as inseparable from civic rights.

Solon was called to power in a crisis of distress (*cir.* 594 B.C.). Throughout Attica the farmers could not pay the debts for which they had pledged their lands and sometimes their bodies to the larger landowners. Solon cancelled these debts, re-established the free-holders in their lands, and redeemed a number of Athenians who had been sold into slavery beyond Attica. Henceforth no Athenian might pledge his body for his debt. Aristotle says that Solon established justice and the democracy at the same time by placing the whole people in the jury courts and permitting any citizen to bring cases of oppression before them. So the punishment of injuries became the affair of all; and with the possession of the justice of the city, the people attained to partial political control. They elected magistrates and called them to account on leaving office. Provision was made for the admission of industrious foreign residents to citizenship. Yet much ancient and aristocratic authority was left untouched; the democracy was by no means completed.

After Solon came more trouble, bringing the dominance or tyranny of Peisistratus and his sons, whose rule was neither base nor cruel. Yet any despotism emptied Athenian life, as it would the life of any real Greek city, of its chief active interest, politics. That was not to be endured, and Cleisthenes, with his people's party, won back the power and established a constitution more broadly democratic than Solon's.

The Athenians, those who lived in the city as well as those who dwelt on the land, were not yet completely and drastically unified. Peisistratus and other leaders of the recent time of turmoil were leaders of their clan, which might be one of the old Ionic tribes in which the people of Attica had been immemorially divided. The strong ties of blood and family lived and ramified within these ancient tribes, to which the natural allegiance of such clansmen clung. If the people and their leaders were to feel and act as Athenians, as the people of one corporate and living city-state, these distracting ties must be weakened and these tribal allegiances annulled.

Hence the fundamental change made by Cleisthenes was a distribution of the four Ionic tribes into ten new ones, and the whole town and country into a much larger number of neighbourhoods or working demes. The latter took over local functions, and became important as the working groups through which should be realized the duties and privileges of a common Athenian citizenship.[1] The deme kept the register of citizenship, collected taxes, and saw to it that a proper quota of its men should present themselves for the juries, to make up the six thousand called for by Cleisthenes' constitution. Afterwards Pericles kept up their numbers still more effectively by providing a day's wage for every juryman.

A permanent administrative body was the Council, established by Solon, and from the time of Cleisthenes numbering five hundred, fifty from each tribe. The Councilmen, like the jurymen, were taken by lot from the contingents chosen by the respective demes. The Council controlled the finances of the city, which became miniature imperial finances after the middle of the fifth century; it

---

[1] See A. E. Zimmern, *The Greek Commonwealth*, Part II. chap. vi. (1911; 2nd ed., 1914), to which these pages are much indebted.

also arranged for the selection of magistrates, including the ten generals, by lot or by election as the case might be. The most influential of these generals might remain in Athens, like Pericles, who as " general " directed Athenian policy for thirty years.

As a result of the constitution, itself energized by the spirit of the Athenians, a large proportion of the citizens of Athens were employed upon the public business of the state, even when Athens was, comparatively speaking, at peace; for she was scarcely ever quite at peace with all her world. One may repeat that Athens never followed an exclusive policy, like Sparta, but from time to time opened her citizenship to foreign residents within the borders of Attica. These residents, even when not full citizens, were loyal and self-sacrificing for the city whose liberal policy had closely knit their prosperity to hers.

The impulse or compulsion of circumstances had never been absent from the causes making for the development of the Athenian constitution. But thought, discretion, and free determination entered and fashioned each part and made them into an harmonious whole. The establishment and the growing prosperity and stability of such a state hung upon the courage and intelligence and rational self-control of its citizens; hung upon those civic and human qualities depicted in the Thucydidean speech of Pericles over the Athenians fallen in the first year of the Peloponnesian war. A more tragic proof lies in the downfall of the Athenian State, which came so quickly when the Athenian democracy failed in intelligence and self-control and gave itself to lust of conquest.

Athens rose to conscious strength from the defeat of Persia ; she then, according to the necessities of the situation and her opportunity, built up her sea-power and a compact empire, consisting mainly of her fellow-Ionians on the Aegean Islands and the coasts of Asia Minor. Her revenues enabled the majority of her citizens to devote themselves to her service, in the government of the city and its empire, on the juries, in the fleet and in the army. She was strong in her walled city and the long walls joining her to the sea and to the unrivalled navy with which she ruled and policed it. Above all, she was strong in the bravery and energy and intelligence of her citizens. Sparta and her allies could not have defeated her, had she not cast herself away in the Syracusan expedition, attempting conquests absurdly beyond her strength. So she broke her citizen army, lost her ships, made new enemies, and entered the path of downfall.

She had been blessed with councillors exceptionally wise. The statesmanship of Pericles seems to us flawless. Athens was wise enough to re-elect him to power for thirty years and follow his counsels. Perhaps the strain of wisdom had been too much for her—for any democracy ! for any sovereign people ! At all events, on committing her fortunes to such as Cleon and Alcibiades, she quickly wrecked herself. Here was her corporate unwisdom.

Athens was only the centre and apex of Greek intelligence. The other little city-states fought with each other and their poverty, and within themselves as well. Each one in accordance with its circumstances and its opportunities, its courage, intelligence, and self-control—or lack of these qualities—built up a government and constitution which seems in no instance to have been an exact replica of any other. In the politics of each Greek city, under the pressure of a penurious environment, or stepping briskly with opportunity, one discerns the Greek intelligence working in some sort of freedom. The variegated constitutional history of the Greek cities is a convincing exemplification of the at least partially free working of the human mind in history.

III

ROMAN JURISPRUDENCE

Seeking further illustration of the action of human ingenuity in fashioning political institutions, we pass from Greece to Rome. There the earlier centuries of political growth terminated in the dominance of a Senate. Originally composed of Patricians, it came to include Plebeians, as these made good their claim to share in the various magistracies. It was not an hereditary body, and yet its aristocratic sentiment continued unimpaired by the admission of citizens who, through their wealth or family, or their abilities, had been elected consuls or praetors. It was thus recruited, under the supervision of the Censors, from the surest bearers of the Roman tradition as well as from the best political and military ability in Rome. If it represented in fact an upper class, the conditions of the recognition and existence of this class made it the best in the community. To the close of the Republic the Senate embodied the energies and qualities of Rome, and maintained a steady continuity of Roman policy.

But turning from the constitutional history of Rome, let us take an illustration from the Roman law, and note some of the incidents of its expansion into that system of jurisprudence which underlies the best legal intelligence of Europe and America.[1]

[1] It is historically unjust to pass over the remarkable body of private law emanating from Babylonia, with its ample foundations set in the code of Hammurabi, the conquering and restoring king who reigned in the twenty-fourth century before Christ during a period of commercial activity. His code was copied and recopied for some fifteen hundred years, as appears by Babylonian and Assyrian tablets. It represents a more voluminous and complex body of private law than is contained in the Laws of the Twelve Tables, and may have been as logically arranged. Both codes require formal modes of contracts, which in the Babylonian code were drawn up by a notary upon clay tablets, and deposited in a temple. Beyond formal requirements, both codes permitted

To begin with the Twelve Tables. According to the current view, this fundamental code was drawn up by the Decemvirs, and finally promulgated in the year 449 B.C. Livy says that a Commission had been sent to Greece to study the " inclitas leges Solonis " and Greek laws and customs generally. Athens was then coming to its height of power and repute, and Livy says that the Commission brought back the " Attic laws." Evidently the intention was to make use of the Greek wisdom in this code which should wisely embody, or revise, the laws and customs obtaining at Rome.

The laws of the Twelve Tables [1] are couched in the form of general imperatives, which open thus : " If one summons [another] to court, let him go." Strict in their formal requirements, they are broad and liberal in their tenor. They sanction a complete freedom of contract between living parties, and the right to dispose of property by will. " When one binds himself or makes a purchase, as the tongue shall have declared it, so let it be "—" as a *paterfamilias* shall have appointed by Will, so let it be."

freedom of contract, and enforced the terms agreed on. The Babylonian code has been published and republished and extensively commented on. Its contents are conveniently given in the article (by C. H. W. Johns) " Babylonian Law," in the eleventh edition of the *Encyclopaedia Britannica*.

Babylonian Law made the basis, if not the substance, of much of the law of the eastern Mediterranean, and so affected Roman jurisprudence.

[1] They are given in C. G. Bruns, *Fontes juris romani antiqui*. I have used the fourth edition, of 1879.

F

The formal modes for contracting must be adhered to. For instance, in a sale the purchaser, before five witnesses, declares the slave or other object to belong to him *ex jure Quiritium*, " purchased by this copper and copper scale "—and with a piece of money he strikes the scales held by the *libripens*.

If legal rights thus formally acquired are to be enforced, it must be by an action in which with corresponding strictness the proof tallies with the demand. The procedure was designed to bring the contention to what in English or American law is called an issue, where a definite statement is made on one side and denied by the other.

This was excellently accomplished by the old *legis actio sacramento*, in which each party engaged to make good his allegation, or forfeit to the State a sum of money deposited in a sacred place. The proceeding began before the Praetor, and advanced to the stage of formal pleading and denial, accompanied by a deposit of the sum to be forfeited by the loser. The cause was then sent to a *judex* or bench of *judices* to be heard and determined.

The early law provided no execution against property ; but its ferocious logic as to the debtor's person is well known. If a controversy was decided for the plaintiff, the debtor had thirty days in which to pay. If he failed, the creditor might lay hands on him and take him again before the magistrate. Unless payment then was made, the creditor could take him to his house and keep him there for sixty days in chains, furnishing him a daily ration. On the three last market days within this period, he could hale his debtor before the praetor and proclaim the amount of the debt. Then if no one paid, the creditor could kill the debtor, or sell him beyond the city, as no Roman might be held as a slave in Rome. If there were several creditors, the debtor might be divided into as many parts. One may suppose that usually the several creditors would have preferred to compromise among themselves. Subsequently, this ultimate rigour of the law gave way before provisions for levying execution on the debtor's property. Yet the consistency with which the law of debt was carried out, gave earnest of the logic which later should be applied more humanely to the adjudication of controversies.

The laws of the Twelve Tables were drawn up for the citizens of a crude and vigorous state, whose views and experience scarcely extended beyond its rather narrow boundaries. But in the following centuries Rome became the pivot of the world; and her genius for affairs and for the rational determination of controversies, in fine, her genius for law, began to build a broad and universal jurisprudence around and about the early law. There had been consideration in the statement and arrangement of the Twelve Tables, marking the beginnings of a jurisprudence. Jurisprudence was to be the great achievement of Rome, and most truly her own, although she drew from foreign as well as native sources the materials for her legal reasoning.

As Rome grew, and wider and more diverse controversies were settled there, not only among citizens, but between citizens and foreigners, or among the latter, a larger consciousness of legal propriety or justice stirred in the minds of those called on to administer the law in the particular case. This consciousness began to express itself in statements of general principles of legal right, and in the endeavour to adjust actual controversies in accordance. Jurisprudence consists in this steady endeavour of the reason to formulate useful principles, and decide particular legal questions in accordance with them, and to enunciate new rules in harmony with the body of the existing law. It seeks concord, order, and system.

Every great people has its special aptitudes. The Romans had a genius both for government, and for the development of private law, which administers justice between individuals. The due administration of private justice is the surest support of the government which directs the affairs of state, domestic as well as foreign. Under the later Republic and the Empire, Rome became the social and political centre of the ancient world ; and if it was not the chief commercial centre, being the capital rather than an emporium, it was the place where all controversies, commercial as well as political, were, in the last resort, heard and determined. The Roman jurists were trained and broadened by Greek philosophy and by the study and comparison of the laws of the Mediterranean peoples. They made good use of their native wits, of their education, and of the experience brought by their opportunities. The result was the most comprehensive body of law and the most admirable jurisprudence ever produced by a people.

" The great jurisconsults of the Empire, working upon the prior labours of long lines of older praetors and jurists, perfected a body of law of wellnigh universal applicability, which throughout was logically consistent with general principles of law and equity, recognized as fundamental. The latter were in part suggested by Greek philosophy, especially by Stoicism as adopted and modified at Rome. They represented the best ethics, the best justice of the time. As principles of law, however, they would have hung in the air, had not the practical as well as theorizing genius of the jurisconsults been equal to the task of embodying them in legal propositions, and applying the latter to the decision of cases. Thus was evolved a body of practical rules of law, controlled, co-ordinated, and, as one may say, universalized through the constant logical employment of sound principles of legal justice." [1]

The second and third centuries after Christ mark

[1] This is quoted, with a little change, from chap. xxxiv. of *The Mediaeval Mind*, where I tried to make a brief statement of the sources of the Roman law. I may use the substance of some of its paragraphs, without further remark.

the time of the law's highest development, when the most eminent jurisconsults flourished. Their " responsa " were authoritative, as decisions of actual cases in the imperial court, of which they were members. More especially the opinions of five of them, Gaius, Julian, Papinian, Ulpian, Paulus, were recognized as of the highest authority by Justinian's *Digest*, compiled from such " responsa " three centuries later.

Looking to the sources, and considering the complex modes of growth of the Roman law, these jurists distinguished the *jus gentium* from the *jus civile*. In the time of the Republic, it had become necessary to recognize a law for the many strangers in Rome, who were not entitled to the protection which her *jus civile* afforded only to her citizens. The edict of the *praetor peregrinus* covered their rights, and sanctioned simple modes of sale and lease, which did not observe the forms set by the *jus civile*. This edict, renewed and amplified from time to time, became the chief source of the so-called *jus gentium*, to wit, liberal rules of law which ignored the peculiar formalities required by the law of Rome. Probably the edict recognized the foreign laws or commercial customs of the Mediterranean peoples; and a study of them led to a perception of elements common to the laws of different peoples. In course of time, the *jus gentium* came to be regarded as consisting of universal rules of law which all peoples might follow naturally.

The judicial recognition of informal contracts rests on the principle of giving legal effect to the intention of the parties. Such a principle, with a knowledge that similar laws might obtain with different peoples, fostered a conception of natural justice. This could not fail to spring up in the minds of Roman jurists educated in a Stoical philosophy which had so much to say of human reason existing among all men. The idea of a *naturalis ratio* was in the air, and these jurists began to treat the *jus gentium* and the *jus naturale* as identical.

Thus, rules conceived as belonging to the *jus gentium* or the *jus naturale*, and representing rational principles, impressed themselves upon the development of the *jus civile*. The jurists applied them effectively to broaden and rationalize the whole Roman law. Judge and jurist learned when to disregard the formal requirements of the older and stricter Roman law, and found ways to recognize what was just and expedient. So the demands of *aequitas* were met, which is a progressive and discriminating legal justice. Law (*jus*) might be identified with *aequitas* conceived as the *ars boni et aequi*.

Roman jurisprudence was finally incorporated in Justinian's *Digest*, promulgated in the year A.D. 530. It was a codification of the *responsa* of the ancient jurists, using their very words, citing their names, and never speaking in the language of Justinian's time. It opens with statements of those general principles which, as already said, might have hung in the air but for the power of the Roman legal genius to apply them to the concrete case. *Jus est ars boni et aequi*—what a wealth of significance has gathered around these words! Again, other famous words : *Justitia est constans et perpetua voluntas jus suum cuique tribuendi*—" Justice is the constant and unceasing will to render each his due (his *right*, his *law*). The precepts of the law are these : to live honestly, not to injure another, to render each his own. Jurisprudence is . . . the science of what is just and unjust."

The second of these passages may be taken as an expansion of the first. Both expressed the most advanced and philosophic ethics of the ancient world. Further exposition follows : " *Jus* has different meanings ; that which is always *aequum ac bonum* is called *jus*, to wit, the *jus naturale* : *Jus* also means the *jus civile*, that which is expedient for all or most in any state. And in our state we have also the praetorian *jus*."

This passage indicates the course of the development of the Roman law : the constantly growing core of specifically Roman law, called the *jus civile* ; its continual equitable application and enlargement, which was the contribution of the praetor, the chief judicial magistrate of Rome ; and the persistent application of the *aequum ac bonum*, noticed in legal rules common to many peoples, but more surely emanating from the reasoning of jurists instructed in the best ethics and philosophy of the ancient world, and learned and practised in the law.

We pass to certain general, but distinctly legal, rather than ethical, rules collected in the *Digest*. " The laws cannot provide specifically for every case that may arise ; but when their intent is plain, he who is judging a cause should proceed *ad similia*, and thus declare the law in the case." [1]   This states the general principle that new cases should be decided logically, and in accordance with established rules.

Sometimes, however, legal incongruities may be found in a statute or in some rule made for a special exigency. They are not to be applied to other cases : " What has been accepted *contra rationem juris*, is not to be drawn out to its consequences " ; or, again, " What was introduced not by principle, but at first through error, does not obtain in like cases." [2]

Such principles make for the consistent development of a body of law. Observe the scope and penetration of some other rules : " Consent, not cohabitation, makes a marriage." This goes to the root of the whole conception of matrimony, and is the starting-point of all subsequent law upon that subject. Again : " An agreement to perform what is impossible will not sustain a suit." This

[1] *Dig.* i. 3, 10, and 12.   [2] *Dig.* i. 3, 14, and 39.

is still a fundamental principle of the law of contracts. Again : " No one can transfer to another
a greater right than he would have himself." [1] The
last is likewise of fundamental validity, but, like
other rules of law, subject in its application to the
qualifying operation of other rules.

Much private Roman law came from the enact-
ments of the people or the rescripts of emperors.
Yet the chief means and method of its development
lay in the declarative edict of the praetor and the
trained labour of the jurisconsults. In these appears
the free constructive intelligence of Roman jurisprudence, a jurisprudence matchless in its rational
conception of principles of justice rooted in a philosophic consideration of human life ; matchless also
in the carrying through of such principles into the
body of the law and the decision of each case. One
will scarcely find a more apt example of the freedom
of the mind working in the creation of civil institutions.

IV

RETROGRESSION AND CHANGE

During periods of what is called advancing
civilization, men build up the political fabric.
When this ceases to draw so large a proportion of
their energies, they may turn more to trade or
commerce, handicraft or art, or philosophy. So it

---

[1] *Dig.* L, 17, 30, 31, and 54.

was in Athens as the fourth century before Christ
passed into the third. And so it was at Rome,
when the Empire had succeeded to the Republic,
and there was little to develop an effective political
character and little scope for the exercise of free
political energies. During the first centuries of the
Empire, responding to the complex growth of
private business, the Roman private law reached
its culmination. Apparently the Empire prospered
exceedingly. Conditions of private human living
had never been as favourable and as assured as
they were within the Roman Empire from the time
of Augustus to the reigns of the Antonines.

Yet even before the close of the second century
A.D., the higher energies of life were weakening. In
Rome they began to pass with the passing of those
energies and functions which make up the seething
content of civic freedom. The intellectual desire
for knowledge lost its force ; the various branches
of literature showed decadence. Domestic and
business activities still functioned, but not the
more strenuous public energy, from which those
in the end must draw support.

Evidences of decay became clearer in the third
and fourth centuries.[1] Political confusion, military

---

[1] One may see with one's eyes an illustration of this
change in the Arch of Constantine, which still stands near
the Roman Forum. It is partly made of robberies from
older monuments, and in part its decoration is the work of
the craftsmen who put it together. Compared with the
older work, belonging to the time of Trajan, the later work is

disaster, more lands left uncultivated, industry and commerce stagnating. There was little credit and a lack of money. Emperors debased the coinage to pay their troops. Taxation had become insupportable. Very noticeable was the decline of industrial freedom; men no longer could follow their bent, pursue the vocation they preferred. Artisans and shopkeepers were bound to stay where the government enrolled them for taxation. Labour was oppressed with penury and over-regulation. The impoverished land no longer bore its crops. The populace of Rome itself had become debauched and pauperized through free bread and circuses. In other cities, the property of the well-to-do was " commandeered " for like demoralizing objects. Through the provinces, in the municipalities, public officials were bound to offices which had become onerous; they were even forbidden to travel, lest they escape from the service of the government. Their burdens descended from father to son.

Meanwhile, as the energies of civilization waned within the Empire, barbarism waxed both without and within its boundaries. Instead of the Roman civilization conquering new provinces, and making Latins of their inhabitants, the invading or infiltrating barbarians were persisting in their barbarism, and were barbarizing the " Romans " and

---

degraded and barbaric. A full explanation of the causes of this decline in art would explain much besides; but it is not forthcoming.

their institutions. A diminishing population left fewer people to bear these increasing burdens.

There had been a gradual lowering of vitality— loss of civic energy, loss of intellectual energy, and finally loss of commercial and industrial energy. The Roman civilization had lost its vigour, its power of propagation. The deeper spiritual or biological or pathological causes of this veritable human decadence still await a discoverer.

Evidently diminished freedom of action had resulted from a lessening of mental energy. As the minds of men became less vigorous, the power of every individual to direct his outer life and occupation declined with the loss of vigour at the source. Nothing is more generally true of the phenomena of " The Fall of the Roman Empire " than that men had become less free in those perturbed and driven centuries. This affords another proof—from an opposite angle—of the mighty agency of the mind in history : loss in all modes of human freedom, mental and physical, follows upon a loss of mental vigour, that is to say, of those qualities which function in freedom, and produce or increase it.

Yet the impulse toward freedom continued not only in these difficult fourth and fifth centuries, but in the still harder and more squalid material conditions of the early Middle Ages. The refuge was of course an inner freedom, not energizing strongly perhaps, nor turning into outward action, but Quietistic, if one will. Young and vigorous

epochs do not seek this inner freedom, since partly
consciously and partly unconsciously, they are busy
working out their free lives in the world. In the
third century before Christ, when the Greeks had
lost the mastery over their political fortunes, and
no longer lived in free city-states, the more thoughtful among them turned to philosophy, especially to
Stoicism and Epicureanism, which are philosophies
of inner self-reliant freedom and inner peace, with
acquiescence in the order of the outer world.

But between the third century before and the
third century after Christ, the tempers and moods
of men had changed. Men no longer relied upon
themselves to attain their goal of inner peace;
they had come to look for it from God. This was
true of the latter-day pagans, as well as of the
Christians, who were increasing in number and
perhaps in influence; for Christianity had spread
through all parts and provinces of the Empire,
before Constantine turned officially to Christ.
Stoicism had itself become almost a religion, a
praying system. Pagans, who were not philosophers,
were beseeching all the gods with a renewed and
relatively hysterical religiousness. The Christians,
in ways according with their varying mentality—
their education, their enlightenment, or their
simplicity—looked for their salvation to Christ and
to the growing host of saints which for them had
displaced the pagan demons.

Evidently men would seek their inner freedom

through different means and under very different forms from those prevailing before the Christian era.   It was an inner freedom sounding in the peace and assurance of religious faith ; and gradually the Christian way of gaining it swallowed up all the rest.

This way was monasticism or the more extreme asceticism of the anchorite, who dwelt as a religious solitary.   Its beginnings reach back to the fourth century, when the Syrian and Egyptian deserts began to fill with monks and hermits.   From the East the movement travelled westward, where monasticism took its general form from the Regula of St. Benedict of Nursia, who was founding the Monastery of Monte Cassino at the very time when the Emperor Justinian in Constantinople was promulgating the great *Digest* of the Roman law that goes under his name.[1]   Until the thirteenth century, when the Orders of St. Francis and St. Dominic were founded, all varieties of western monasticism were modifications or developments of the Regula of Benedict.

Our reference to monasticism is confined to pointing to it as a refuge of peace and freedom. To be sure the monk lived in strict obedience to the rule of his Order and the commands of his Superior.   But his might be the securest freedom of the undisturbed religious life, the life of faith,

[1] A.D. 529 or 530.   For a sketch of the origins of Monasticism I must refer to chap. viii. of my *Classical Heritage of the Middle Ages*.

devotion, and possibly of loving ecstasy—the last, perhaps, more frequent among the sisterhoods of nuns. So the monk, driven by the evil conditions of the world, and by the peril of his soul, won the inner freedom of the spiritual life, in some respects a substitute for the freedom of the old Stoic within the fortress of his will.

One may also bear in mind that the monastery offered greater actual peace and security from outrage for men and women than could be found elsewhere in the mediaeval centuries preceding the thirteenth. Early in that century the Orders of the Franciscans and Dominicans were founded. In them monasticism and the inner freedom of the spiritual life went forth from the cloister into the world. Some connection may be seen between this coming of a more actively ministering, preaching, teaching, travelling monasticism and the rather more secure conditions of life abroad in the wide world.

Our illustrations have been taken from the ancient world because of the naked simplicity in which they present themselves, due, of course, to our relative ignorance of the web of complex influence surrounding, permeating, and affecting them. Yet they may safely be taken as true examples of the working of the free intelligence in the shaping of human institutions, political, legal, or social. Throughout history, modern as well as ancient, all manner of influences, suggestions, impulsions, or necessities have joined in fashioning institutions, besides the frequently tricked and thwarted conscious intention of the mind. Nevertheless, the factor of human ingenuity is never absent, and usually devises the form. Moreover, in the case of those political institutions through which the governed in some way control the form of government and direct its operation, it is clear that such " free " institutions depend for their growth, efficiency, and strength upon the free energies of at least certain portions of the people and their capacity for self-government. It is also clear that such institutions cease to function, and even to exist, as the political energies of a people dwindle, and their political intelligence, their faculty of deciding aright, their rational self-directing power of self-control, fail them.

This seems always true, while at the same time we recognize that untoward circumstances — for example, a tyrannous *force majeur*—may prevent the growth of free political institutions; and likewise that a *force majeur* may overthrow or destroy them ; or they may lose their efficiency or even cease to function when a situation becomes too large, or too self-willed, as it were, and irresponsible, for their application. The political forms of the Roman Republic may have been unsuited in themselves, and too inelastic, to provide a proper government for a subjugated world. The Republic could have governed itself but not the world ; and could no longer govern even itself when demoralized by the opportunities and temptations of world conquest. An imperial reorganization was needed, and the despotic power of a single ruler.

And, alas, as human beings multiply, as trade and industry increase, and human affairs in general become stupendous and immense, the intelligence and self-directing self-control of human kind, or of the individuals conducting public business, do not grow greater in proportion to their task; and so fail, and confusion ensues. This thought has come to many doubting minds since the Great War. The memory of this catastrophe may also serve to remind us that sometimes there rise waves of group consciousness, heightened and angry convulsions of herd instinct or national feeling, that may act as *force majeur* upon men, quite overwhelming their free decisions. Politics, domestic as well as international, only too often exhibit the compulsion of a situation and the *force majeur* of events. For the time this may submerge the free intelligence and judgement even of the intelligent individuals among the people, and all are hurled along in one turbid torrent.

We refrain from following our illustrations down the centuries to our own times. Most readily they could be found in the history of England and the history of the United States of America. But the antique world was very rich in human nature. The examples of its politics and its political per-

sonages have constantly enlightened later men.
Witness the immortal *Lives* of Plutarch ; and the
reader of Thucydides' *History of the Peloponnesian
War* might easily conclude that the English statesmen, say of the eighteenth or early nineteenth
century, drew their political maxims from it. So,
perhaps, we need not follow any further our political
illustrations of the free action of the mind.

CHAPTER III

I

PARALLELS AND DIVERGENCIES OF THOUGHT

FROM the partly free and partly determined growth
of institutions we turn to still loftier and possibly
less constrained conquests of the human mind. In
the fields of religion, philosophy, and science we may
look for its most complete freedom. While review-
ing the contributions of one people and another
and of great individuals to these attainments of
humanity, some historical order will be observed.
Yet, until we approach the modern time, it will not
further our merely illustrative purpose to divide
our matter into its possibly three mighty provinces
of religion, philosophy, and science. Life and history show no sharp boundaries between the three.
Like imaginative literature and art, they are phases
of the spiritual and intellectual progress which in
its entirety responds to the totality of human

faculty, or to the wholeness of the human mind. The final criterion of the value or validity of any particular product or instance of religion or philosophy or science has always lain in the response or reaction of other faculties or parts of man to the action of the faculty which is operative ; or, conversely, in the responsiveness of that faculty and its product to the reasonable insistence of the sum of the balanced faculties of man acting in their corporate union.

Thus the religious impulse, or the predominantly religious mind, must, in the end, justify itself before the court of the other human impulses and rational faculties. Philosophy, likewise, will seek to adjust itself with the imperative religious impulse. Nor can philosophy for long ignore the action of the scientific mind proceeding constructively through close and systematic observation of the natural world with ingenious experiment and verification. And natural science, with its tentative hypotheses and experimental methods which disclaim all knowledge that cannot be verified, may feel limited and narrow and insufficient, may be conscious of a pressure toward metaphysics to supplement its intermediacy, and even feel the temptations of religion ; it may recognize that it is no complete and adequate creed for man, since man is other than a scientist, even as he is other than a philosopher or a saint.

Not every man is saint and philosopher and

scientist; many a man is not even one of these !
But the full gamut of humanity includes them all
and needs them all for its grand harmonies.

It may be doubted whether men were free discriminating agents in the savage beginnings of what
should become religion, philosophy, or science.
Human environment everywhere presents some
like features, some like suggestions. The sun and
moon rise and set in all lands and the stars appear ;
there is everywhere a change of seasons ; everywhere injury and disease come upon men, and men
have cause to fear ; everywhere they are nourished
and protected in childhood, and eat the fruits of
earth ; everywhere they yearn in desire, beget,
bring forth, and nourish. Thus they receive some
like enlightenment, and have something of the same
rude sense of the facts of life. Hence it is that like
mental processes and parallel conceptions appear
everywhere. Savage ethical notions have a general
resemblance, and everywhere men project their
crude self-consciousness into the outer world, and
imagine its occurrences to be as acts of things alive.
Everywhere men have worshipped the sun and
moon and their own ancestors, and have buried
food and utensils with the dead, failing to conceive
of any complete cessation of bodily need and
function. Very strikingly they have everywhere
used, and indeed still use, perforce, the analogies of
physical qualities and relations to help themselves
to turbid spiritual concepts, in which the dregs of

matter gradually settle downward, leaving the spiritual more clear.

We may infer that, through these early stages, confused and slowly clarifying thoughts arise from natural suggestions—the suggestions of the human environment and of common ways of living. Very gradually and slowly will human thinking begin to free itself from the compulsions of early need and the universal suggestions of circumstance, and evince some intellectual and volitional discrimination. Therewith a more palpable individuality arises among men. For one may note that wherever discrimination and ingenuity appear, they are the discrimination and ingenuity of an individual, are, indeed, of the essence of individuality. The herd, as a herd, is neither discriminating, originative, nor free. Freedom and discrimination are of the individual, the salient individual.[1]

Strikingly will this appear in those most salient individuals, those great men who fashion the knowledge, virtue, and ideals of mankind. The founders of religions, poets, philosophers, discoverers, and men of science lifted themselves from the cradle of the world and became creators of what was new

[1] Speaking comparatively. It is accepted to-day that throughout the whole organic world no two individuals of even the lowest orders of plants and animals, and not even any two cells, are absolutely like. So no two human beings. But in the text I am referring to that more salient individuality from which come thoughts and acts noticeably different from those of other members of the tribe.

and what was better. With them the mind worked
free, though often building better than it knew.
These men were themselves in their self-directings,
supreme individuals ; they were also the sum of
prior human development, which made the ground-
work of their loftier constructions. Each was as
the *apex mentis* of his age, and the accumulated
energies of life and thought wrought in the action
of his mind. His own discriminations, his free
determinings and constructions, in adding to the
intellectual and spiritual faculties of men, made for
the enlargement of human freedom.

One more point, to keep us from confusing two
different but related concepts. We have argued
for the freedom of the mind, inclusive of the will
as its kinetic or conative faculty. There is no
nobler office of this mental freedom than to liberate
the soul from the bondage of its foolish fears and
give it peace. It is the mind, in its essential freedom, that through increasing knowledge and finer
discrimination works ever for its own deliverance
from fear, thus moving in freedom toward its peace,
its spiritual adjustment with the universe and God.

II

EGYPT, CHINA, AND INDIA

A mass of early crude conception survived in the
practical thinking and terrified or more hopeful

imaginings of the folk of those two fertile river
valleys, Mesopotamia and the valley of the Nile.
Two thousand years and more before the birth of
Christ the changing races of Babylonia, as we have
noted, had built up a material civilization amply
guarded by law, by custom, and royal power. But
their thought of all the powers not human was
wrapped in fear. Spiritually, they were driven and
pursued ; and their vision of the grave was horrible.
So they grovelled before gods and demons and the
plagues with which the superhuman powers smote
men. They developed a complex of astrology, sooth-
saying, and magic, which survived the walls of
Babylon, and passed on to afflict men for thousands
of years. The later Assyrians brought the fear of
God close to the Hebraic stage of its evolution, and
developed an acute sense of sin. Yet throughout
their obvious and sometimes articulate perplexity
they never reached valid moral distinctions. Ceremonial error, or touching the forbidden thing,
brought plagues from the gods as fatally as fraud,
incest, or murder. Scant freeing of the spirit lay
in any Mesopotamian scheme of things.

The magic and religious code of the equally
ancient Egyptian civilization, undisturbed by its
inconsistencies, fabricated an existence within and
beyond the tomb that should be a magically safe-
guarded replica of life on earth. Only Pharaohs
and great nobles might build eternal tombs, and
furnish them with those substantial images and

paintings on which most surely hung the existence
of the dead. Yet gradually a clearer ethics and a
juster faith ameliorated this preposterous scheme.
The earthly righteousness or wickedness of the dead
began to count. The gods began to reward right
conduct as well as punish crime. They became at
last gods of justice and truth. Through virtues
practised on the earth a way was opening for men
of lowly lot to win some existence after death.
Such, too, might purchase things with which the
rich were well equipped : charms to quell the
dangers threatening the dead, and magic scrolls on
which were disavowals of crimes committed before
death. The life to come had become a partially
ethical adjunct to mortality.

So the Egyptians made vague and fluid their
magic and religious scheme, endowing their gods
with pity as well as justice, finding them beneficent,
even loving and to be loved. In heterogeneous
fashion their contributions to human freedom and
peace of mind were to touch the Greeks and Romans.

We pass down the centuries and travel to Eastern
Asia, where the great establisher of Chinese thinking,
Confucius, lived in the sixth century before Christ.
He is a grandiose illustration of the human spirit
deliberately seeking its freedom within a web of
deferential conduct, regarded as the reflex of the
dominating and all - embracing way of Heaven.
" Heaven " meant life's consequential order. It
was just and righteous, since there was no loftier

or more potent standard by which to criticize or judge it. In its all-embracing operation the way of Heaven effected a sufficient reconcilement, almost an identification, of the intelligent human will with the order of the world, including the results of human conduct. The nature, the personality, of Heaven was as broad and as vague as the sky above ; and it held no declarations of the lot of man beyond this life.

The terms of the Confucian statement are themselves vague and comprehensive :

" What Heaven has conferred is called the Nature ; an accordance with this Nature is called the Path ; the regulation of the Path is called Instruction.

" The Path may not be left for an instant. . . . On this account the superior man does not wait till he sees things, to be cautious, nor till he hears things, to be apprehensive. . . .

" While there are no stirrings of pleasure, anger, sorrow, or joy, the mind may be said to be in a state of Equilibrium. When those feelings have been stirred, and they act in their due degree, there ensues what may be called the state of Harmony. This Equilibrium is the great root, and this Harmony is the universal Path.

" Let the states of Equilibrium and Harmony exist in perfection, and a happy order will prevail throughout heaven and earth, and all things will flourish."

These principles, when made explicit in political

and social precepts, ensure correct and reverent ties between ruler and people, among the members of a family and throughout society. Confucius sought to interpret and restore the social and religious laws which he imagined to have obtained in the ancient Chinese Empire before it fell under the misrule of many princes, which was its condition while Confucius lived. He would learn and practise the ceremonial rites and rules of propriety, which are the social reflex of the way of Heaven. Thus conforming his conduct, his character would be moulded ; and he might hope that his teaching and the example of his perfectly adjusted character would tranquillize China.

" At fifteen," says Confucius, " my mind was bent on learning; at thirty, I stood firm; at forty, I had no doubts ; at fifty, I knew the decrees of Heaven ; at seventy, I could follow what my heart desired, without transgressing."

For himself and for his people Confucius reached intelligent freedom of conduct through conforming his will to his conception of the way of Heaven. This was closely related to natural law and ethical sequence, while suggesting the thought of obedience to the will of a vague and impersonal god.

From Confucius we pass to the Indian freeing of the spirit. Two thousand years ago Indian doctrines, impregnated with the Indian temper, spread through vast Asiatic populations far beyond the swarming country of their birth. The Indian

scheme of deliverance from life's chains holds profound human values, although they may not suit
our Western minds.

It was the product of intricate, insistent processes
of thought, impelled by the temperamental Indian
antipathy to the phantasmagoria of the world.
The dialectic was subtle, the metaphysics profound.
And most profound the philosophic human truth
that ignorance is the basis of all suffering, while
deliverance lies in knowledge. But the religious
philosophers of India, viewing the world of nature
through the disaffections of their introspection,
felt no impulse to study it. Contemplating its
phenomena, they investigated none of them, deeming
them but as *Maya*—delusion and temptation. So
they gained no real knowledge of the world they
lived in. Phenomenal life was to them but bondage
to unreality. Their goal was liberation, whether
beyond this liberation lay the blessed Absolute or
Nirvana.

The Indian temperament was one ; and homogeneous were the forms of Indian reasoning and the
method of its superfine dialectic. The philosophic
doctrines of the priestly caste of Brahmans are
contained in the Upanishads. Guided by them,
the enlightened soul might gain knowledge and
clarity of purpose enabling it to dissolve desire and
disentangle itself and its true goal of the Absolute
from the illusions of the world.

In opposition to these doctrines, Buddhism was

a metaphysical revolution. It recognized no
Absolute and no soul that could attain it. There
was no being ; only ceaseless *becoming*, incessant
change. That name and form called man was part
of this becoming. Yet this sentient bit of flux,
through enlightenment and resolve, might win
through to salvation from the chain of causation.
The blessed release from the torture of blind desire
and incessant change was Nirvana. The Buddha
never said whether that was a conscious state or
an achieved nothingness. It was deliverance from
the suffering which all life is. But neither had it
been clear that any consciousness inhered in that
state of final absorption in the Absolute which
Brahmanism aspired to.

So to our minds the two goals are the same ;
likewise the method of reasoning, though with
different metaphysical concepts. Yet Buddhism,
while seeking detachment from desire as earnestly
as Brahmanism, discarded asceticism as a foolish
means. All life was suffering : why add to it ?

Brahmanism had forged the Indian consequential
chain : the binding power of the act done in this
or in a previous life. The good deed or thought
helped the man on along the path of enlightenment
and deliverance. The path itself was a progressive
liberation of the spirit. With each advance, the
man became more free. But terrible was the power
of the act. In Buddhism, this Karma, the power
of the act, became even the bond of continuity

between one life and the next, that is to say, between the present phase and the next of individual becoming. It was a terrific strengthening of the law of consequences in human conduct, consequences which must be lived out and expiated before the portals of release might open.

The iron conventions of the Indian social system in which Brahmanism was bound up impaired its universality and prevented its acceptance beyond India. The Buddha's enlightenment freed him and his doctrine from racial bondage, from the chains of caste as well as the practices of Indian asceticism. Possibly its metaphysics were in clearer harmony with the goal of liberation. It was the form of Indian religion that gained wide acceptance in Thibet, China, and Japan. Even before it went forth from India it had decked itself with the popular idolatries which its founder's strenuous thinking had ignored.

III

ISRAEL

The makers of Indian thought cared no more for the history of their land than for other delusions of the world. History was no delusion, but a sheer demonstration of Jehovah's governance, for the people of Israel, to whom we make a far spiritual flight, in order to observe their so very different

contribution to the advance of human consideration. In the minds of the Prophets, the history of
their people Israel was an intimate and purposeful
leading by the hand of God. Had not Jehovah
called Abraham out of the land of Ur in order to
establish him and his seed for ever in the land of
promise ? Had not Jehovah there confirmed His
promise to Jacob ? and had He not thereafter
delivered Israel from Egypt and brought them back
across the desert by His goodness, and by His power
established them again in their land ?

Afterwards He had raised up judges to judge
them, and kings to rule over them and repel their
enemies. He had taken David from the sheepcote
and made him king, to become the most ardent of
Jehovah's royal servants ; had given him a promise
to maintain his seed after him in the kingdom,
chastening it with many rods when it should sin,
but not casting it off for ever.

Then there had come backslidings in Israel,
idolatries of kings and people, and fiery warnings
from Jehovah's spokesmen. Israel had separated
into two kingdoms, the northern one to become
more idolatrous than Judah and to meet its downfall sooner. Yet after many warnings came that
unutterable calamity of the exile, and the apparent
destruction even of Judah.

It was for the sins of kings and people—of a
surety ! Yet how reconcile the appalling facts with
Jehovah's promises to the patriarchs and to David ?

It was through faith and through consideration of this course of fact, ever becoming more portentous, and from the untowardness of the final calamity, that the unshaken line of Israel's prophets enlarged their understanding of Jehovah's ways with men. Their minds worked large and free, building up a more universal scheme of the divine polity in the world, and, with a heightened spirituality, discerning the fulfilment of Jehovah's promise in no grandiose Palestinean kingdom, but in Israel's divinely appointed mission to mankind.

Mark the stages of the mental and religious progress of these prophets, who are not to be thought of as priests or theologians, but as theocratic publicists, reformers, even statesmen.

Amos is the first whose written message has survived. He belongs to the eighth century before Christ. In origin a shepherd, he was a harsh judge of sin, yet all the while was broadening his conception of justice and universalizing his thought of God, Jehovah is righteous. If He chose Israel for His people, it was not to indulge them in their sins, but to hold them to a stricter account. Jehovah is the God, and the creator, of the heavens and the earth, and ruler over all peoples. His eyes are upon the sinful kingdom of northern Israel to destroy it, but He will not utterly destroy the house of Jacob.

Amos's younger contemporary, Hosea, gives voice to Jehovah's clinging love, which cannot bear to abandon the sinful people : " When Israel was young, I loved him, and out of Egypt called my son hither." If only they will repent, " I will heal their falling away, gladly love them. . . . I will be as dew unto Israel."

Both Hosea and Amos are convinced that obedience to Jehovah will establish Israel in safety and gladness. Since Jehovah rules all nations in the power of His righteousness, it must be that the righteous prosper, obviously and visibly. These two prophets are fixed in this assurance, which needs many qualifications.

In the mighty mind of the younger Judean, Isaiah, monotheism is deepened and further illuminated. He sees the nations as the rods of Jehovah's anger, axes with which God hews. How absurd for Judah to offer Him in expiation anything save faith and righteousness! What madness to rely on Egypt, a broken reed compared with God's weightier rod, Assyria! The horsemen and chariots of Judah are obedience and abstention from idolatry.

Isaiah could not doubt that righteousness and national well-being went hand in hand. But his assurance that Judah will prosper, if obedient, breaks before a realization of the folly of rulers and people, their no-gods and empty rites, their sought-for pleasant answers and wilful falsities—sin upon sin, bringing destruction. Did Isaiah look beyond the impending ruin to a future restoration, when a Prince of Peace should sit upon the throne of David, and to His kingdom there should be no end ? When the king should reign righteously, and the folly of fools should be laid bare, and the eyes of them that see should not be dim and the stammerer's tongue speak plain ? Such a vision glorified the minds of later men, writing in Isaiah's name.

The book of Deuteronomy set the blessing and the curse before the people and each one of them ; would they cleave to Jehovah, or be cast out ? for the time was coming when fathers no longer should suffer for the sins of children, nor children for the sins of fathers, but every man die for his own sin. Pursuing this moral discrimination, Jeremiah foresaw a new covenant, when Jehovah should write His law no longer on tablets of stone, but in the hearts of Israel.

When Jerusalem fell, Jeremiah, or another, wrote that book of Lamentations : " It is of Jehovah's mercies that we are not utterly consumed . . . for He doth not willingly afflict or grieve the children of men . . . let us search and try our ways, and turn again to Jehovah."

This wonderful people of the Jews, or wonderful individuals among them, reached the truest and sublimest thoughts of their God, and of their inclusion in the sure fulfilment of His will, only after He had cast them out in exile. Then more clearly did they realize His ways, and understand His moral law, and perceive His purpose that they were to be His people not for themselves alone, but for the glory of His name and as a light to the nations.

The priest-prophet, Ezekiel, saw Israel's restoration as a people cleansed and sanctified, upon repentance, loathing themselves for their abominations. Others gave voice to the hope of mankind redeemed through Israel, and resolved anew the chequered tear-stained relationship between righteousness and prosperity. These were mysteries, to be reconciled with the universal power and righteousness of God.

In that providential exile, Israel learned, or certain Israelites learned, spiritual wisdom through suffering, and gave wonderful expression to their faith in Jehovah's love. With decades of servitude in a foreign land, the thought came to these partial slaves that it might be as Jehovah's bruised and suffering servant, pre-eminently serving His other servants, that Israel should be redeemed. Thoughts struggled upward of a service of universal mediation, and of atonement through suffering, even for other sinful peoples. With this consecration came assurance of forgiveness, and of Jehovah's peace and presence in an Israel, redeemed, restored, and sanctified through service and atonement. If Jehovah had bruised His servant, making him to bear the guilt of many, He, Jehovah, had been afflicted in all the afflictions of His people, and so had drawn His servant within His passionate redemptive purpose of suffering, the suffering that

shall make many righteous. Magnificently and
with a tumult of exultation, these thoughts are set
forth in exilic portions of the book of Isaiah.

In intimate comfortings, the servant holds to
God, is enfolded in His presence. Within the scope
of this assurance lie his peace and freedom. But
it is the Psalter that, supplementing the visions of
the prophets, utters the many phases of sorrow and
inalienable comfort filling the consciousness of man
before his God, and voices the manifold realization
of the relationship between God and man :

Like as the hart which panteth after the water-brooks,
So panteth my soul after thee, O God.

For countless millions, Confucianism was to be
a rule of life, a way of freedom within a voluntary
harmony of beneficent observance ; India, through
the intense disgust of its high thinkers for the
changing world, and their goal so difficult for us
to think, was likewise to afford a way to freedom
for countless millions. In Israel the prophets held
themselves the spokesmen of Jehovah ; they were
not conscious of acting after their own judgement
or the decisions of their own free will. Yet how
had God delivered His commands to Elijah ? Not
through the violent wind or crashing storm or earthquake, emblems of force, but in a still small voice,
the symbol of persuasion ; and Elijah's response
lay in voluntary obedience. In reality, under divine
suggestion, the Hebrew prophets follow their free

intelligence. So the Psalms utter the ardent religious desire wholly to submit the singer's will, nay, his whole being and desire, to God. The human will seeks refuge in the will of God, but still voluntarily.

IV

GREECE

It was the lot of Greece to assemble the free energies of man, insist upon both the action and the value of the full round of human faculty and trait, and test each element of life in the crucible of thought. No other people used with such free discrimination their self-reliant minds to ascertain and establish the elements of human well-being; and no other people, through consciously advancing thought, proceeded so clearly to select the best. They seem to create a harmony of beauty, wherein that which was most fair should show in its true human dignity.

The Greek conception of human well-being, of happiness, was that which Plato realized, and Aristotle expressed in final analysis. It consisted in the free and unimpeded exercise of human function, leading on to the attainment of man's furthest actuality, the most complete fulfilment of himself. Before Aristotle spoke or Plato lived, many a Greek had lived out this principle according to his impulses and dominant desires, with such

discrimination as was in him ; or had achieved it
in the expression of beauty and wisdom through
art and poetry ; or had seen the goal of its fulfilment along the way of knowledge and reflection.
It meant the actualization of the manifold contents
of life.

The manifold of Greek life drew unity from the
Hellenic temperament and the recognition of
Hellenic principles. Yet the divergent impulses
within this manifold were keenly felt and ardently
pursued. Life's different phases were beautifully
expressed in actual achievement, or in words or
sculpture. Let us consider the controlling unity
and then the types of diverging impulse and
attainment.

From the first clear expression of the Hellenic
genius in the Homeric epics, the Greeks appear
pre-eminently endowed with the faculty of reason :
not the dialectic metaphysical faculty, which created
the philosophy of India, but a faculty as broad as
life, and equipped with keen perceptions of all things
taking place on earth, yet focussed always upon the
greatness and the mortal limitations of men. The
epic heroes, Achilles or Odysseus, never cease to
reason or to present in reason their conduct and
resolves. The gift of reason, and the habit of
reasoning plausibly or fairly, persist through all
Greek life and literature.

These clear perceptions and this gift of reason
were possessed by men vibrant with desire. Eagerly

and passionately the Greeks desired life, its full
content, its gladness and exultings, its successes,
the beauty of its endeavours and achievements ;
and they were endowed with curiosity ; they wished
to know. Their nature was intellectual.

Perception, reason, a searching intelligence
illumined Greek desire, checked it or urged it on,
moulded it, and through rational guidance raised it
to objects most truly and nobly human. Reason
marshalled the objects of desire according to their
value in human life, and thus brought order and
proportion to the individual life whose desires were
its springs of action.

Impulsively as well as with their minds, the
Greeks loved beauty, beauty of form, beauty of
language, beauty of conduct. The love of beauty
pervaded Greek life and thought. It permeated
the whole round of desire included in the Greek
nature ; it joined with the Greek reason, and conformed to the guidance of the Greek intelligence.
Thus made part of the Greek reason, the love of
beauty became ordered, whole, consistent, intellectual. It formed the final element in the pro-
portionment of all things desirable ; it emerges as
life's harmony and perfection, co-ordinate with the
good. The thought of beauty as fitness, proportion,
pervaded Greek principles of conduct, fashioned the
famous motto μηδὲν ἄγαν, nothing too much, and
entered the finely conceived virtue of σωφροσύνη,
which is the temperance of wisdom.

A consideration of the evil opposites of this beautiful quality brings us to the core of Greek ethics. They are ἄτη and ὕβρις, the pride which is thoughtless and irrational, lacking justification in the nature and condition of man. This insolence of folly leads to injustice and brings overthrow; the sail of the unjust man shall be riven, and he shall perish on the reef of justice. Ὕβρις transmits itself as a curse, as an infection in the blood, which shall work itself out in new ὕβρις and in crime on crime. This is the teaching of Aeschylean tragedy.

We here touch the Greek law of consequences. The innocent may be involved; but through expiation of their inherited blood-guiltiness they may find peace. They shall exemplify the truth, from suffering, knowledge. The thought of σωφροσύνη and of the catastrophes springing from its evil opposites joins with the conception of the divine law of Zeus: for it is Zeus's law to cast down the proud man who has sinned, and his overweening children; but suffering shall bring wisdom to those who act aright, and they shall not be utterly cast down. Man's freedom of right conduct is to respect justice, and avoid overweening insolence and folly. Thus living, he will keep within the guard of the divine law. Say the chorus in Sophocles' *Oedipus Tyrannus*: "May destiny still find me winning the praise of reverent purity in all words and deeds sanctioned by those laws of range sublime, called into life throughout the clear heaven, whose father

was Olympus alone . . . the god is mighty in them,
and he grows not old."

The types or phases of the Greek spiritual
achievement and contribution to the human
heritage of free creative thought are neither dis-
connected nor disparate. They are related to each
other in the interplay of Greek impulse and the
Greek unison of rationally proportioned desire.
At one extreme is the heroic deed, at the other the
pursuit of wisdom.

Heroism, with the Greeks, was not a thing of
brawn, of brute courage, or even of impulsive
irrational devotion. Courage and resolve, great-
heartedness, were indeed essential and pre-essential,
but the Greeks required the concurrence of the
mind to rationalize and so moralize the act. In
Homer, besides ἀρετή, which is valour, πινυτή, which
is *prudentia*, consideration, makes part of the heroic
character. So does the sense or quality of αἰδώς,
which is honour, with its complement of shame at
all things shameful. Assuredly heroism sounds in
character; yet Greek heroism, at least, was illumined
by thought and guided by consideration. This is
true of the Homeric Achilles, and always evident
with Odysseus. Some centuries later the victory
odes of Pindar make clear that the value and
beauty of the heroic deed lies in its accord with
thought, its fitness to become a theme of song.
Hence it is that Pericles, in his speech over the

Athenian dead, emphasizes the rationality of their conduct, showing how justified by reason and inspired by consideration was the patriotism of those who had fallen for their city. Their conduct was not blind or even impulsive, but sprang from the freely working intelligence.

The qualities of heroism must be such as will submit to the proving of consideration. So thought the Greeks; and as we follow the creations of Greek art and poetry, we realize how rational they are, how they unite with the *idea* in their consummate beauty. This is as true of the architecture of the Parthenon as it is of the sculptured forms which adorned it and made clear its meaning; it is as true of the odes of Pindar as of the dramas of Aeschylus and Sophocles.

And now, if Greek heroism must be such that it might be invested with thought, and make part of the rational scale of life; and if architecture, sculpture, and poetry shall likewise meet the loftiest exactions of the mind, and present life whole with due consideration for whatever element should touch this lyric poem of Pindar or Archilochus, this drama, say, of the house of Atreus, or the subjects of that frieze with which, as with a coronal of life's attainment, the Parthenon is bound; if so, then, in accordance with these principles, the Greek pursuit of knowledge should sound in all the interests of human life, and proceed through an ever more perfect appraisal of them all.

Greek philosophy starts from the wholeness of life. Its masters sought the fulfilment of the whole rational man, including everything which the mind might approve. Yet wisdom, which is assimilated knowledge, was the freest, the most distinctively human portion ; in itself it yielded satisfaction, and without it the rest of human happiness could not be had, or, if quickly grasped, would prove fleeting.

Greek philosophy was a free unfolding of the human spirit. The mind of man lifted itself up in freedom and addressed itself to observation of the world, with speculation as to its nature and processes, and then turned to the mind itself and to the elements of human well-being. Freely the Greek intellect searched for the truth of what satisfied the mind, for what was good, for what was real, and for what was beautiful. It was a quest for knowledge, a lover's pursuit of wisdom. It became a testing of all things.

The first philosophers, citizens of Miletus, an active-minded Greek city of Asia Minor, devised hypotheses to explain the nature and origin of the physical world. Thales, geometer and astronomer, conceived the original substance as water. His hearer, Anaximandros, looked still to the fecund moisture of the air, and thought of man as something like a fish in the beginning. A follower of his conceived of world transformations through rarefaction and condensation. Like them seeking

the reason for the things about him, Pythagoras, of
another city, discerned how essential were numerical
relationships.[1] " Nature loves to hide," declared
Heracleitus, and sought to track her through those
myriad changes in which strife might be attune-
ment, and destruction might be procreation. All
things are in a flux ; they seemed to him as a vast
fire-transformation.

" Nay," said Parmenides. " There is no flux.
All is being, and changeless as an eternal sphere."
Still other was the thought of Empedocles, with his
famed four elements, and two more besides, Love
and Strife, to make them unite and separate.

Thus these Greeks tried to think the world,
spurred by the difficulties observed in each other's
systems. They had reached a conviction of order
and of natural law holding unswervingly throughout
the world. But the active physical factors were
still too ponderous. So Anaxagoras hurled *Nous*
into the fray, as the more agile agent of formative
creation. Substance is pregnant ; its innumerable
small elements hold all things, implicit, not yet
unfolded. But *Nous* is infinite, and self-ruled,
unmixed with all of these. It starts them on their
ordered revolutions, through which things as we
know them gradually assume their forms. *Nous*
had not yet become sheer immaterial mind. But

[1] The Pythagorean thought that everything is number
has, of late years, become less enigmatic and more full of
meaning.

it is on the way—on the way to the conception of
the divine mind and will as the creator and regulator
of the universe.

A physical hypothesis was destined to counter
this conception, and, as its opposite, in some way
maintain itself even to our time. This was the
theory of atoms, infinitely numerous, indivisible,
of every shape, yet indestructible, and having ceaseless motion. Men's souls consist of fiery atoms
having the liveliest motion. The great Democritus
accepted this theory, and co-ordinated it with
human life, admirably humanizing his philosophy.
His vision would include all things, and penetrate
all. He distinguishes between " primary " and
" secondary " qualities in objects, and between the
convincing apperceptions of the atoms of the soul
and the confusions issuing from the atoms of the
senses. Turning his rational knowledge into a
way of life, he evolved a finely spiritualized ethics,
in which knowledge, virtue, happiness were at one.
" Happiness and misery are of the soul "—" From
understanding proceed good counsel, unerring speech
and right conduct." Intention is the criterion of
good or bad acts : one must will no wrong. Knowledge is better than the riches of the Great King ;
and the whole earth is open to the wise.

It might well be, and it was already seen, that
all these grand hypotheses of origins involved inconsistencies. No one as yet had tested the processes and pitfalls of thought itself, though Zeno

had propounded certain conundrums of logic, which since his time philosophers have solved in various ways. The Sophists now assumed their educational rôle, disclosing many puzzles. Their dialectic brought self-consciousness to Greek thinking. Close upon their tracks, more earnestly and more constructively, Socrates took up the testing of thought. Keenest of questioners, he conducted his inquiries so that they should lead to better conceptions. Aristotle places to his credit the inductive method and general concepts or definitions —a credit huge enough! Through his method and his definitions, he strove to reach laws of conduct valid for all men, because founded on conceptions true for all. So he made his escape from the Sophistic exaggeration of the relativity of thought. True knowledge, moreover, must produce right conduct : since no one errs, or sins, willingly. Carrying on the humanism of Democritus and the Sophists, Socrates, as Cicero says, called Philosophy from the heavens, and established her in the abodes of men, set her upon the study of man.

The sublime mind of Plato has been often metamorphosed in the writings of his imagined disciples and eager interpreters. We scarcely need to add our word. Still we must recall some of the conclusions with which he extended the realms of human thought and made firm the assurances of the mind's freedom, and, if one will, unshaken peace.

The topmost needs of this rich nature, and the

field of its lasting joy, were held in its metaphysical
energies. Its masterful insistency was as to the
reality of mind and the validity of concepts mentally
visualized. These were tested, if not formed, by
an argumentation, destructive or constructive,
sometimes whimsical, but always carried forward
by a creative imagination.

No single argument compassed his whole conviction. The "Platonic Idea" has proved the
most influential form assumed by his insistence
upon the absolute reality of spirit, verily of things
spiritual. The mind contemplates the universals
in all things, perceives them everywhere. Plato's
type-ideas, from existing solely in the mind, pass
out beyond, and are beheld as absolute spiritual
entities, and as the creative shaping powers of
objects of sense-perception, which are their images.
The idea of the Good, with which most closely joins
that of the Beautiful, is the noblest and most real
of all, the most absolute of ideal prototypes, as well
as the most universal creative power. It becomes
as God, at once the fashioner of the world and the
measure of all things.

Obviously that which in man is most real, and
may approach nearest to its prototype, is the mind
or soul. Its health, its well-being, its blessed
happiness is to mirror and realize within itself
beauty, justice, goodness, the excellence of every
noble type-idea. Herein is the soul's noblest action ;
herein it creates its freedom and its blessedness.

The soul which clings to the opposites of these ideas
of the beautiful and true clings to its ill, to its
disease. Its cure is to be purged of its falsehood
and wickedness. Of course the unjust man cannot
be happy; and of course it is better for a man to
suffer injustice than to do it.

As Plato grew older he held with increasing
certitude that the world was ruled by mind. God
created it because He was good, and wished to create
after His likeness; and God gave the world a soul.
The world-soul and the souls of men are immortal.

The mind of Aristotle soared less sublimely;
but, more universally than Plato's, it ranged the
regions both of phenomenal and metaphysical
existence. Clearly he stated and demonstrated that
the fullest freedom of human action, the best
activity for man, the fulfilment of himself in the
attainment of his final end and actuality, consists
in the life and action of the mind. The mind's
highest function, its loftiest self-realization lies in
the consideration of the ultimate causes of existence,
which are the noblest objects of thought. From
this ultimate contemplation, true and distinctive
human activities slope downward, broadening to a
base of virtues which find their roots in character
and conduct, and likewise have their end in the
perfecting of character and conduct. The whole
plan of human life thus issues in power from the
noblest focus of action of the free intelligence, and
radiates through expanding zones of knowledge to

its still free and active outer actualization in right conduct.

The Aristotelian εὐδαιμονία, well-being, happiness, embraces the fulfilment of the whole human nature, even those phases of life which man shares with other animals. It includes the active virtues. Following Plato's last ethical conceptions, Aristotle conceived virtue as the conduct which avoids excess, and adheres to the mean, in conformity with the conduct and opinions of the best men.

Aristotle contributed to human progress this plan of life, wherein the mind should find its noblest happiness in the consideration of loftiest matters—even as God the great Contemplator contemplates that which is most worthy, which is Himself. This human plan likewise embraced the fulfilment of the well-ordered residue of life. Aristotle's intellect, to the enduring advantage of men, entered and enriched every field of knowledge. Great in metaphysics, he was also the creator of formal logic. He wrote upon the Soul or Life of man, and its faculties and manner of perception. He was a great biologist, pre-eminent as a classifier of organisms and as a comparative anatomist and embryologist. His work on *Ethics* was rightly admired by future generations; his work on *Politics* exerted enormous influence; and his *Rhetoric* and *Poetics* were to prove notable. Only perhaps in physics and astronomy he failed to adopt, or rather to foresee, those views of Greek astronomers which, two thousand years later, Copernicus proved to be the best.

The prodigious expansion of Greek philosophic thought ended with Aristotle, although after him came astronomers, physicists, mathematicians who presented the best knowledge of these high matters that the world was to have for two thousand years. But metaphysical speculation seemed tired. Systems suited to a less self-reliant time were needed—old-age philosophies. The most significant of these was Stoicism, which no longer regarded knowledge as a final end and a fulfilment of human nature, but as a means to a true practical ethics having human happiness for its end. As an old-age philosophy Stoicism had narrowed to a direct desire for the soul's peace, which some of us still think may be won more surely through the full activity of the highest energies of the mind.

Reason is man's essential nature, said the Stoics ; and human reason is part of universal law, which is God all-ruling, all-permeating, and moving everything. Conduct directed by the will in accordance with right reason, human and divine, is virtue. That is man's sole good and happiness. Emotions should be controlled ; pleasure and pain are indifferent.

Stoicism was to become more broadly and warmly human than this cold basis might suggest. We are approaching Roman times, the epoch of the merging of separate states and provincial views into the cosmopolitanism of the Hellenic-Roman Empire. In these surroundings Stoicism, from its philosophic recognition of the unity of the world and the oneness of pervading law, warmed to a conviction of the common brotherhood of man. Recognizing the beneficence of the divine purpose it became more ardently religious, became a praying system of philosophy. Broadly and benevolently it developed the thought of a justice which should embrace the whole brotherhood of man. It contributed much to the ethical temper of the world. Yet it failed to perceive the changing and relative character of justice ; failed to perceive the essential relativity and invalidity of a conception that must change with social conditions ; failed to recognize that the absolute principle is love, and that, for man, love represents the law, the will, of God.

Yet the just intention, the will to act justly, continues as the progressive righteous principle. In the end it must transform itself into that absolute principle which abides and cannot be done away, though it may be instructed with advancing knowledge. This is love, the desire, even the yearning for another's welfare, or for the welfare of all, coupled with the will to promote it.

From many sides this had been partially discerned before it was embodied in the Gospel of Christ. And there had also come conviction that justice, and love at last, carried the assurance of his own welfare to him who was just—as Socrates had seen, and Plato. Prophet and Psalmist, their faces turned toward God, knew that in God's love of His servants, and the servants' yearning and efficient love of God and neighbour, lay the servants' surest salvation. Then came the supreme law of Deuteronomy: "Thou shalt love the Lord thy God with all thy heart and with all thy soul and with all thy mind, and thy neighbour as thyself." Christ took up the same, poured His heart's blood into it, and died for love of God and love of man. The conclusive final statement is Paul's "For we know that to them who love God all things work together for good." Looking back to Stoic principles, which are put more dumbly, this statement is just as inevitably true. No harm can come to him who is in accord with the natural moral law, and in ardent harmony with the will of God.

V

Hellenism and the Gospel

We return to our course of historical illustration. Each age stands on the shoulders of the past, though sometimes its feet slip painfully. This is but the law, or sequence, of cause and effect, or continuity. With respect to certain eventful epochs this principle has been set in a phrase, "The fullness of time." If we knew better the antecedents of Confucius we might see more clearly how he stood on the shoulders of the past, and drew strength from its impulses and attainment, as well as from the demands of his own age. Even the supremely great man seems in the line of human development —though the next generations may slope sadly downward from his height. It was thus with Gotama the Buddha, and it was so with Jesus.

But the great man is of supreme importance as a human or divine achievement. He and his value are not exhausted in his apparent effect either upon his own time or on times to come. Sometimes this effect and lack of effect is startling and perplexing. The person, the words of Jesus, have been as strength and ineffable comfort to millions ; yet the faithful historical student may look vainly for the tangible moral effect of Christianity upon the Roman Empire. The level of conduct remained much as before, only declining with the decline of civic strength and virtue. Nevertheless, the crucified Saviour was marvellously accepted by His time ; while former, possibly stronger, epochs might have been in other mood. One queries whether Jesus would have overwhelmingly appealed to Socrates and Plato, or to Confucius. One can imagine Socrates putting difficult questions to Him, which doubtless He who replied so wisely respecting the Roman tribute money would have answered wisely.

As we all know, the spiritual condition of the Roman Empire was adapted to the reception of

Christ's Gospel when it came. Intelligent men were no longer finding satisfaction in rational investigation ; they, too, with the unthinking millions, were looking for religious assurance, looking even to gain some sort of salvation. Stoicism had become as much a religion as a philosophy ; and from Asia Minor, Syria, and Egypt emotional religions swept the Empire. The cult of the Great Mother Cybele came from Phrygia, and the orgiastic rites of Attis, with their symbolism of a resurrection. From Egypt came Isis, Osiris, Serapis, and many gods from Syria. From Persia came Mithraism, a strenuous dualism and a soldier's faith. Many of these were presented in the guise of secret " mysteries," through which the votaries shared the power and immortality of their god.

Indeed, Graeco-Roman paganism in all its forms was becoming more emotional. One finds the tendency in the poets Virgil, Horace, and Juvenal. A little later, the Stoicism of Seneca, Epictetus, and Marcus Aurelius becomes progressively prayerful. Many austere pagan figures moved through the Empire, urging men to a better realization of their nature, teaching them that thus they might be saved from the evil of the world. That quite wonderful final system of Greek philosophy, known as Neo-platonism, drew within its compass and rational patronage the yearnings and tendencies of the centuries which even then were turning to the gospel of Jesus.

Neo-platonism was the creature of metaphysics and mood. Plotinus, who died in the year A.D. 270, was its chief creator, an austerely yearning spirit and a great metaphysician. Elaborately he set forth his system of the emanation of life or being, from the *Nous* to the world-soul and the souls of men. His mind was incited by the desire for ecstatic well-being. He looked to a supra-rational union, through ecstasy, with the Absolute One. The system was ascetic in principle, theoretically despising the flesh.

The followers of Plotinus were less nice in their quest for salvation from the vile confusion of mortal life. The more strenuous held to his conception of the flow of life from the Absolute One through the *Nous* to the world-soul and the souls of men. But they raised themselves to the level of this argument by curious mediatorial means, and used all manner of magic rites to repel the myriad demons which must be dispersed before the true god could enter his temple.

The reasoning and the mood of Neo-platonism pervaded the Christianity of St. Augustine, the great Pauline Father of the Church, who with such difficulty had cleared his reasoning, but not his spirit, from Manichaeism. That was a malignant eastern dualism, largely of Persian origin, which as a heresy was destined to cling to the skirts of mediaeval Christianity, till, a thousand years later, it was overwhelmed in the blood of the Albigenses.

It was a younger sister of the drastic heresy of Gnosticism, which had threatened to deform Christianity almost at the beginning. Gnosticism had carried all manner of heterogeneous Hellenic and oriental elements. It was dualistic, writhing with a sense of contamination, full of devils, looking for salvation in passionate sense modes, or through mystic processes. It was a bastard Christianity, which would not accept salvation from the God-man, nor admit the reality of His manhood or that He really died upon the cross.

Cast into such a world, the Gospel of Jesus, the mighty reasonings of Paul, were like to suffer change as they won their way to acceptance. Indeed if we look to the third and fourth centuries, we see that Catholic Christians, Arians, Gnostics, Neo-platonists, and Manichaeans have much in common with each other, being all held in the current moods and acceptances of that period. But Christianity had dynamic and living qualities by which it rose a victor over its contemporaries, although rather indelibly affected with their characteristics. It drained them of their vital elements, accepting asceticism for example, and clothing both the need and the means of salvation with a more human and divine reality.

Indeed large parts of the later history of Christianity still have to tell of the gospel of Jesus and the doctrine of Paul struggling through the web of their early entanglements with orientalized Hellenism.

Nor may we suppose that Jesus Himself, and Paul, were not involved in the opinions of the world in which they lived, for example in regard to demons and their casting out. Yet the heart of life within their teaching was their own.

The Gospel of Christ's life and teaching was a new power in the world. It held the highest principles of conduct, and revealed their divine sanction in the immediate and eternal blessedness of the person receiving and fulfilling them. Its precepts and assurances were endowed with the life and power of Christ.

The prophets were the background of Jesus. He fulfilled the law and the prophets with a spiritual fullness that meant abrogation of ritual and special commands and racial limitations. More intimately he fulfilled the characterization of Jehovah's servant in the fifty-third chapter of Isaiah. Under every stress Jesus' words and acts responded to His highest self; and no human life has passed beyond the range and guidance of His utterances. Both to His disciples and to future generations His personality suggested divinity, of which He appears to have been conscious.

Christ's life and teaching were at one. His life was spent within the compass of a single motive, to do His Father's will. It was a human copy of God's righteousness and love; it was man in the image of God.

Each one of us seeks to bring his life to harmony,

to unity. Our impulses spring from our individual
natures ; and our intellectual faculties, however
they extend their range, are still rooted in ourselves.
The oneness of a human life must work itself out
within the singleness of a purpose broad enough to
include and direct the man's fullest understanding
of the best. But every one feels his weakness, his
mortality, his creaturehood. His own endeavour
is his contribution ; but attainment depends on
much beyond him. To inspire his endeavour he
needs hope, even assurance, that his purpose shall
not fail of realization. The higher and broader his
purpose the more must he have faith in the co-
operation of some power corresponding to the
highest conceptions of his mind. In fine, he must
rely on God. Through faith in God and the conformity of his purpose to the divine will a man's
life gains its complete unity.

Jesus exemplified this principle, that only in
God can a man be at one with himself ; and so fully
and universally did He exemplify this that after
Him no man might seek to unify his life, and move
on toward its accordant fulfilment, without approaching Jesus. " No man cometh to the Father but by
Me," He says in the Gospel of John.

All great interpreters of Christianity have thus
sought to unify their lives through Christ in God.
They have also recognized as fundamental the
principle of self-sacrifice for the Kingdom of Heaven's
sake, which is a sacrifice leading to attainment. He

who seeketh his life shall lose it ; he who loseth his life for My sake shall find *it*, his own life completed and rendered perfect. Christ asks no man to give himself up for ever; but through sacrifice of self to fulfil and attain himself in the eternal will and purpose of God. To sacrifice one's self for the Kingdom of Heaven's sake is to reach that full accord and relationship of man to God, which is the blessed fulfilment of human life.

Many foolish things have been said of the baseness of a faith which looks for a reward in the life to come. But it is no alien reward which Christianity offers as a bribe. Rather that which shall come to the righteous believer is the sheer fulfilment of his nature, the issue of his working faith. To destroy this hope were to cut the continuity of life's development, divorce action from its results, impugn the moral law of consequences.

Christ's gospel set forth no scheme of barter, nor any system of measured justice. It was love running to meet love : man's love realizing God's love of man, running to accept it, and obey it and fulfil it. Love is also commanded among men as the bond and principle of life. Men are brethren because sons of the same Father. They shall adjust their love of fellows to the requirements of God's universal and imperative love, which seeks ever the well-being of His creatures. There is no command to love dotingly, or foolishly, or lustfully. Man shall love his fellow as himself, to his salvation, not to his perdition. In this sense he must try to fulfil the difficult mandate, " Love your enemies, and pray for them that persecute you, that ye may be sons of your Father which is in heaven."

The figure of Jehovah's Servant and the figure of Jesus are both reflected in the " Beatitudes," which delineate the Christian lot and character. Blessed are those who are poor in spirit, who hunger and thirst after righteousness, who are merciful, pure in heart, peacemakers, and persecuted for righteousness' sake : theirs is the Kingdom of Heaven ; they shall obtain mercy, they shall be comforted, with righteousness shall they be filled ; they shall see God and be called the sons of God.

Christ brought God close to man—not a sparrow falls to the ground without your Father,—nay, the very hairs of your head are numbered ! His life was a manifestation of the relationship with God which His words and acts set forth for His disciples. He taught no special mode of living, prescribed no fixed rules, set no limits to the full development of human individuality, provided it proceed in righteousness and unto the Kingdom of Heaven. The gospel afforded universal scope for life. It demanded a free choice, free obedience, and love freely given. It was a call to the exercise of the human intelligence and will in perfect freedom. A man must be born again, in the spirit of perfect freedom. " The truth shall make you free."

The gospel of John discloses the spiritual height

and depth of this freedom in which man shall walk clothed with the truth of God. Through the truth he has entered into life ; in the truth he hath eternal life. " And this is life eternal, that they should know thee, the only true God, and Him whom thou didst send, Jesus Christ."

" And the glory which thou hast given me I have given unto them that they may be one, even as we are one ; I in them and thou in me, that they may be perfected into one ; that the world may know that thou didst send me, and lovedst them, even as thou lovedst me."

It was not easy for man to attain the height and breadth of freedom, human and divine, presented by the Gospel. No one won his way to it with grander or more congenitally hampered genius than Paul. The Epistles to the Romans and Galatians reflect the tortuous arguments by which he had disentangled his feet from the fetters of the law in his struggle to attain the freedom of Christ. By the power of his religious genius, or through the revelation within him, this Pharisee reached the thought of Christ as the measure of the stature of the full-grown man, and became convinced that in Him was the fullness of the Godhead. In that Godhead which was in Christ will Paul live and move and have his being—and eternal life : " The free gift of God is eternal life through Christ Jesus our Lord."

Likewise through his grand humanity and his

religious genius Paul comes to his wise thoughts
of charity in conduct and observance, and to his
sense of love the best of all—the love of brother,
the constraining love of Christ, the love of God
which is our life and our assurance, since " we know
that to them who love God all things work together
for good."

VI

The Middle Ages

The gospel of Christ was the freeing of the human
spirit proffered to mankind.   Through its transforming power a man or woman might become,
like Paul, a new creature in Christ Jesus.   Yet the
world of man, on their side, transformed it to the
measure of their understandings.   As we all know,
the modes of accepting and (God save us!) practis-
ing Christianity make the religious and the main
intellectual history of Europe until the opening of
the modern age.

The first manner of authoritative acceptance of
Christianity by the Graeco-Roman world involved
its formal transformation into the categories of
Greek philosophy and Roman Law.   Only through
these modes of thinking, to which they were
accustomed, could the educated men of the Roman
Empire receive the Gospel.   Accordingly the Greek
and Latin Fathers of the Church, bending to the
needs of their own processes of thought, translated

the Gospel into dogmas formed in the moulds of
Hellenic philosophy and Roman law. In such
forms, and at the same time trailing the current
superstitions of the age, the Gospel passed over into
the Middle Ages.

In the meanwhile a decline in the ancient civilization had taken place, and what is called the Fall of
the Roman Empire. The courses of the material
and intellectual phenomena of this decline and so-
called Fall have been studied, and may be found
set forth in many books. Intellectually the world
seemed tired, its energies relaxed and degraded.
Why, we do not know.[1]

We pass on into the early mediaeval disintegration and prospective regathering of the elements of
civilization, and to the coming of fresh energies
making for a renewed progress toward freedom.
One must not think that the savage or the barbarian
is free. He is more tightly pinioned by his customs
and superstitions, and by the pressure of his needs,
than his civilized brother is by laws and social
conventions. The social freedom of man comes
with the expansion of his mind and the attainment
of a better order.

The Middle Ages present a novel emergence of
humanity. They have been converted to Christianity, and about them lie the *disjecta membra* of the
ancient civilization ; or the old knowledge is held
in scrolls which only gradually may be unrolled and

[1] Cf. *ante*, Chap. II. iv. p. 74 *sqq.*

understood. Mediaeval progress lies through the vital appropriation of Christianity, through the recovery of the antique knowledge, and the reactions upon it of the mediaeval mind, and through human growth.

The Middle Ages received, and gradually made their own, the Christianity of the Church Fathers, with the Gospel still breaking through and stirring men's hearts. This patristic Christianity was in the main a construction of the mind. It had not yet become incorporate in the lives and emotions of men and women. But the Middle Ages received it from a revered and greater past. It was sanctioned by the saints who reigned above. As years and centuries rolled by, men learned to understand it, and made it their own. Its commands, its threatenings, and its promises had long been feared and loved. " Its persons, symbols, and sacraments had become animate with human quality and were endeared with intimate incident and association. Every one had been born to it, had been suckled upon it, had adored it in childhood, youth, and age. It filled all life ; with hope or menace it overhung the closing hour."

There was little for the Middle Ages to add to the dogmatic structure of their religion. Intellectually they could but rearrange and apprehend anew. Their true religious function was the emotionalizing of the religion which they had received : their renewal of the Psalmist's outpour of his soul in fear and love before his God, their acceptance and living understanding of Jesus' close communion with the Father, their expression of their utter love for Him that died for them, and of their terror before His coming at the day of Judgement—such was their supreme contribution to the riches of the human soul, and to the freedom of its love of God.

Monasticism had come to the Middle Ages from the early Christian centuries. With fervour they accepted it as the type of the perfect Christian life. After St. Benedict had so wisely drawn up the basic regula, one great monk after another added to the rule, or re-adapted it to meet the corruptions and fervour of his own time. In and through this life of celibate devotion to the bridegroom Christ, generation after generation of monks and nuns poured forth the ardours of the spirit, the heart's blood of their souls. Their lives, their words, their love and tears and pity, deepened the reality and enriched the consecration of man's communion with God, of humanity's unison with the divine. As an institution, monasticism was the outer form within which the zealous Christian soul pursued its peace and freedom.[1]

The deepening knowledge and better understanding of the Latin literature may be followed from the ninth century onward. Scholarship progressed with the stabilizing of order and the growth

[1] Cf. *ante*, p. 78 *sqq.*

of social life. There were always men who loved
the classics. But Petrarch and Boccaccio in the
fourteenth century possessed broader learning and
had attained a somewhat more level-eyed and urbane
appreciation of Livy, Cicero, and Virgil than any
mediaeval humanist before them. Partly mediaeval
in their tastes, they were middle terms between the
Middle Ages and the coming time—twin morning
stars of the strong revival of letters in the generations which followed them.

The later mediaeval period enlarged its thoughts
of law and justice through a study of the Roman
law as presented in Justinian's Digest ; and from
the time of Aquinas the *Politics* of Aristotle, with
its analytical tableau of civic constitutions, became
part of the political consciousness of Europe.
Through the genius of the same Aquinas, and the
labours of his preceptors and successors, the Aristotelian encyclopaedia of philosophy and natural
knowledge was recovered, and in part was worked
into the scholastic system of Christian theology.
These great productions of the ancient world were
comprehensible to this mature mediaeval period,
and in turn educated and strengthened it.

Like all philosophies and theologies, mediaeval
scholasticism may be regarded as a search for truth
and an endeavour to state it. But the primary
truth for scholasticism was the truth which saved,
and the same was held in authoritative revelation,
that is to say in Scripture, in its dogmatic translation

into creeds, and in its authoritative interpretation by the sainted Church Fathers of the fourth and fifth centuries.   The Fathers, among whom Augustine was supreme, inherited the concepts of Hellenic philosophy and Roman civil institutions.   Augustine felt the Gospel of Christ; he made his own the contents of Paul's Epistles; but he reasoned in the categories of Greek philosophy and after the composite manner of Latin rhetoric and Roman law.

The writings of Augustine and other Fathers carried antique conceptions and the antique vocabulary into scholasticism. Outside of the patristic vehicle, certain scraps of antique knowledge and fragments of Greek philosophy passed over into the Middle Ages, furnishing the elements of education and presenting the rudiments of philosophic discipline and a nucleus of questionable natural knowledge.   This intellectual treasure was enormously extended as the more elaborate logical treatises of Aristotle came into use and his substantial philosophy was made known in the thirteenth century.   The former furnished the technical method to be followed in the ascertainment of scholastic truth, while the vast Aristotelian encyclopaedia of substantial knowledge and philosophy set the schematic form and supplied the contents for the mediaeval scholastic system.

Hence scholasticism enlarged the compass of its quasi-investigation in the Aristotelian tomes of

Albertus Magnus and Thomas Aquinas, reaching its culmination in the latter's *Summa Theologiae*. But it rarely looked beyond Scripture and the Church Fathers and Aristotle. The veritable task, grandly accomplished by the genius of Aquinas, was a systematic restatement of the whole possible content of Christian truth, making use of the logic of Aristotle and incorporating such of his substantial material and philosophical conclusions as did not obviously counter the Christian faith. The substance was given, and a logical discipline provided. The harmonizing and constructive genius of Aquinas proceeded through a judicial and catholic comparison of authorities, often enough divergent. With all-considering judgement he selected the conclusion which with far-reaching consistency fitted into the Christian scheme. No pertinent argument was left unconsidered, while every element of possibly accordant truth was drawn upon and used as material in his catholic construction. The august result presented almost the organic unity of the work of a single mind.

Such a work involves much exercise of the mind in rational discrimination. Within determined conditions, the mind might work freely, yet still under the motive or compulsion of presenting and adhering to the truth which saved. The scholastic mind worked toward a goal, with its material given it. Doubtless no philosopher is quite detached from ulterior considerations while he deems himself meditating upon truth. But the scholastics recognized that the vital truths which saved should be for them the criterion of knowledge. Later philosophers will seem freer, less directed and determined in their minds.

CHAPTER IV

THE FREEDOM OF THE MIND IN RELIGIOUS REFORM

THE Middle Ages closed. The human mind fared on, still strong in its endeavour to enlarge the functions of its freedom. With enhanced desire it proceeded to extend the basis of its action in more comprehensive knowledge. The fifteenth and sixteenth centuries carried on the happy task of drawing the classic Greek and Latin literatures again into the lives of men. A clearer consciousness of nationality and of racial difference had come over the northern peoples, leading incidentally to a more passionate disinclination to contribute to the support of the foreign Roman hierarchy. At the same time an embittered sense of social inequality and industrial injustice prepared large masses of people for schism or revolt of any kind. In the Church the ecclesiastical dicta and even the monastic life were losing vitality and power; and renewed and violent efforts broke forth, especially in the mighty personalities of Luther and Calvin,

135

to regain and still enlarge the vital freedom of the Christian man.

This revitalized communion with God was freed from the needless mediation of the priest. Yet it was not more tolerant of divergent types of free belief than the mediaeval church had been. One must distinguish between the soul's freedom of direct communion with its God, in which the mediaeval saints also had lived, and liberal toleration of unacceptable opinion. Within the range of their vital convictions, human beings are rarely tolerant. We are tolerant as to what has become indifferent, or as to which our thoughts are vague and lax. To-day we are more liberal in religion than in our polemic over our material welfare. It was not so in the Middle Ages, when religious convictions might be lurid ; nor was it so in the sixteenth century when Luther and Calvin lived, and wars of religion drove peace and prosperity from France.

Whatever was the deeper cause, a vigorous freeing of the religious spirit followed upon the enlargement of knowledge in the fourteenth, fifteenth, and sixteenth centuries. This larger knowledge had been won by the energies of individual minds seeking a surer enlightenment and a better truth ; through a closer study and appreciation of the Latin classics, and then the Greek ; through a more adequate understanding of the Hebrew and Greek text of Scripture ; and through fresh investigations in the fields of physics and philosophy. Undoubtedly a broader knowledge of the classics and a truer understanding of Scripture in Hebrew and Greek, were direct antecedents of the religious reform, or revolution, in Germany and the Low Countries, Switzerland and France. Stimulated by the example of Petrarch and the host of Italian humanists in the generations following him, classical studies had shown some advance in these countries during the fifteenth century, and in the sixteenth flourished exceedingly.[1] Johann Reuchlin, born in 1455, established in Germany, under persistent persecution from reactionaries, a veritable knowledge of Hebrew ; in France the inspiration of improving scholarship set men to thinking of a purified and reformed religion ; in Switzerland the zeal of Zwingli was the fruit of humanism working in a stalwart and reforming personality.

Pre-eminent through his reasonableness, the breadth of his humane and religious interests, and his great literary facility, was Erasmus of Rotterdam (1466–1536). He was not as learned a Grecian as his rival, the Frenchman, Budé, but his writings worked more widely to spread a love of the classics in France and Germany and England. With tireless interest he re-edited the works of Jerome and Augustine, and crowned the labours of his Christian scholarship with an edition of the Greek New Testament (1516). Almost all men, even scholars, were

---

[1] Cf., generally, chapters vi.-xvii. in my *Thought and Expression in the Sixteenth Century.*

until then satisfied with the Latin Vulgate. The idea of going behind it, with an appeal to the original Greek, was revolutionary. Erasmus' Greek edition awakened great interest—Luther himself began to restudy the New Testament in Greek; it aroused also vehement disapproval, as virtually impugning the authority of the Church, which held the Vulgate sacrosanct. But as a true advance in critical scholarship, it had come to stay.

Other works of Erasmus, his *Praise of Folly*, his *Colloquies*, both of which passed through multitudes of editions, opened men's eyes to the cheats and follies of daily life and the abuses then infecting the Roman Catholic religion. By these satirical writings, which might be witty or might be mordant, destructive or morally improving, he disposed the more intelligent to view all life, as well as religion, reasonably, and to reject what was absurd. Though he drew back when the explosion came, no one had done as much as he to prepare men for the reformation of religion.

Luther was led up to and prepared for politically as well as spiritually. In the century before his birth a strengthening consciousness of nationality and differences of temper and mentality among the peoples of Europe were threatening the unity of the Roman Catholic Church. Spaniards and Italians, for example, on the one hand, Germans, Netherlanders, Englishmen on the other, were not of like religious tempers, and were no longer a docile herd

of sheep for the spiritual shepherding and temporal
fleecing of one papal Church.   The enforced though
willing habitation of the papacy at Avignon through
the great part of the fourteenth century broke the
political catholicity of a Church palpably under
French influence, if not becoming French.   Spiritually as well as politically the papal Church suffered
further irretrievable damage from the Great Schism,
which began upon the return of Urban VI. to Rome
in 1378, and lasted till 1417.   Thereupon had come
Council upon Council—of Pisa, Constance, Basel—
endeavouring to heal the Schism and subject the
powers of the Pope to the decrees of Councils.   The
Conciliar Movement failed to achieve the latter
object, not because the Popes were too powerful,
but because of secular and political dissensions
between Spanish, French, German, and English
ecclesiastics.   A reaction followed, and the Church
became again a monarchy, ruled by a papal Curia
which for all secular and most ecclesiastical purposes was Italian.

To Wyclif, the great Englishman and keen
reconsiderer of Church doctrine, the papacy while
still at Avignon was a foreign cormorant Church,
and when the Schism broke out, it became to him
a cursing two-headed Antichrist.[1]   Wyclif was a
free and clear-thinking theologian, reformer, and
publicist ; of great energy, having an undaunted

[1] See *Thought and Expression in the Sixteenth Century*,
chap. xix.

and unhushed spirit. His radical attitude as to the Eucharist and priesthood was accepted by John Huss, the Bohemian whom the Council of Constance burnt. A century later Luther said, "We are all Hussites without knowing it"; and his career paralleled that of the first and greatest of English reformers. But the religious temperaments of the two men differed, and because of the richer fecundity of his nature, and a riper situation, Luther's revolt had vaster results.

It was as a German that Luther revolted from the Roman papacy. His address *To the Christian Nobility of the German Nation* covered all the complaints voiced by the *Centum gravamina* against the papacy, of the very Council of Worms from which Luther went forth an excommunicated heretic. To Luther and a large part of his German nation the Roman papacy was a vampire that sucked good German blood. Intolerable papal abuses, chiefly the abominable sale of indulgences, drove him to post his Theses on the door of the Castle church at Wittenberg, and enter upon that fierce outer conflict with the Catholic Church through which he reached the certitude of his inner spiritual freedom.

But he reached his inner freedom, which necessarily underlay his freedom of conduct, not merely through the driving compulsions of his conflict with the Church. An inner, if somewhat tumultuous, peace, a freedom from anxiety and a freedom of conduct as a faithful Christian man, had also come

to him through the free judgement of his mind, indeed
of his whole nature ; his intellectual faculties were
inflamed and energized by the religious impulse
which drove on to God, demanding a union through
the intuitions of faith and love, a union in no wise
to be mediated either through a priest or through any
limping, hopeless good deeds on the part of Luther.
If ever the mind of man worked in its essential
freedom, Luther's mind worked free in the preparation of his spiritual manifesto, *The Freedom of
a Christian Man.*

It carried the convictions of Paul ; but the serried
argument of this German sixteenth-century gospel
came from the mighty mind of Luther :

" A Christian is a free lord over all things, and
subject to no man. A Christian is a bounden
servant to all things, and subject to every one."

Opening with this Pauline paradox, it proceeds :
A Christian is both spirit and body. According to
the first he is a spiritual, new, and inner man ;
according to flesh and blood, he is a corporeal, old,
outer man. Hence the Scripture paradox : he is
both bond and free.

In so far as he is a spiritual inner man, no outer
thing can make him pious and free. That the body
is free or the reverse, neither helps nor hurts the soul.
The soul is not helped when the body puts on holy
garb, fasts, or does any good work ; for an evil man
can do all this. Nor is the soul injured when the
body abstains from all this.

The soul needs only the holy Gospel, the word of God preached by Christ. In that word thou shalt hear thy God telling thee that thy life and works are nothing in God's sight, but must perish. Believing in thy guiltiness, thou must despair of thyself, and with firm faith give thyself to God's dear Son. Then thy sins will be forgiven thee through faith, and thou wilt be righteous, at peace, with all commands fulfilled, and free from all things, as St. Paul says.

Therefore the true work for Christians lies in building up Christ and the word within them. Faith alone, without works, makes righteous. Scripture consists in commands and promises. Commands belong to the Old Testament, and bring no strength to fulfil them. The man despairs. But God's promises in the New Testament assure him that, if he will believe on Christ, he will fulfil all and be free from sin and from desire of evil. God alone commands; and God alone fulfils. "Whoever in right faith cleaves to these words of God, his soul is united with them, and the virtues of the word become the soul's, and through faith the soul is righteous, peaceful, free, and full of all good things, a true child of God. No good work cleaves to God's word like faith, nor can be in the soul, where only the word and faith can reign."

Faith joins the soul to Christ. All the good things of Christ become the soul's, and its sins are swallowed up in Christ's invincible righteousness.

Through faith all believers are priests and inter-
cessors, and lords of all, through God's power, who
does their will; they need nothing, and have
abundance—spiritually.

But men are not all spirit; not altogether the
inner man. We are also bodies. Thus the Christian
is the servant of all, and bound to the service of all.
Though justified through faith, we abide in this
bodily life, associating with others. Here works
begin; and the body must be practised in good
works, that it may conform to faith, and not cause
the inner man to stumble. Works must not be
done in the thought that they make the man
righteous before God; but voluntarily and freely
to please God. Just works do not make a just
man; but a just man does just works. Nor do
evil works make an evil man; but an evil man
does evil works.

As towards men, our works must be done in love.
My God has given to me, utterly worthless and
damned, righteousness and salvation through Christ,
so that henceforth I need only to believe that this
is so. I will act toward my neighbour likewise.
Freely must the good things of God flow from one
to another of us. " A Christian does not live unto
himself, but in Christ and his neighbour : in Christ
through faith, in his neighbour through love."

The power of religion dwelt in Luther; the
dynamic sense of man's relationship to God moulded
his purposes and inspired his action. It was as the

energy of God in him, as it had been with Paul and Augustine and Francis of Assisi. Under this inspiration, his mind worked free, building out his conceptions of the all-in-allness of the human relationship to the divine. Yet though his mind worked free, perhaps we may wonder, or perhaps we need not wonder, that he should pour himself out in argument against the freedom of the human will.

Erasmus, late in life, thought fit to enter the lists against Luther with a humane and rational argument in support of the freedom of the will, treating the subject as a matter of philosophical opinion and probability.

In his tract, *De servo arbitrio*, Luther hurled himself against this view. It was most important that Christians should know what the will could do, and how it stood in relation to God's grace. In order to have righteousness through faith one must distinguish as to what is God's work and what is ours. " It is also necessary and salutary for Christians to know that God foreknows nothing casually and conditionally ; but that He foreknows, pre-ordains, and accomplishes all through His unchanging and eternal and unfailing will. This principle, like a lightning stroke, strikes to earth and crushes out free will."

He says at the conclusion of his lengthy argument : " If we believe that God foreknows and foreordains all things, and in His foreknowledge and foreordainment can neither be deceived nor hindered, then nothing can take place that He does not Himself will. Reason must admit this, while it bears witness that there is no free will in men or angels or in any creature."

Reason must bear witness against its freedom ! Luther's reason bore this testimony very freely, very joyfully. If he was chained by the pre-assumptions of his argument, he found his chains of gold, and loved them. When he thought of the ineffable benefits God had prepared for him in Christ, predestination became full of comfort, as he says in his *Table Talk*. So Calvin also was to argue for predestination—the full double predestination of some souls to heaven and the bulk of mankind to hell—and find comfort in it. The arguments of both these great men were suggested, and, as they thought, forced upon them by anterior authority and the premises of their faith. Yet Calvin's mind worked as incisively and as effectively as Luther's, though, one may say, less like a torrent.

It was in Geneva, and from Geneva, that this child of France, with his essentially French mind, built up a Reformed Church and political institutions in harmony. Calvin was in these respects a creator. The Calvinistic church, which in its completed existence was a church-state, proved an organization making for civil liberty in England, Scotland, France, the Netherlands, and the English colonies of North America. In Geneva itself, where

Calvin, through many struggles, emerged an autocrat, he perfected his church-state, under which the people became as effective citizens as they were church members. He directed the codification of the city's laws, and devised an excellent adjustment of taxation ; he proved that interest was not usury, an advantageous economic recognition ; he improved the city's health by the construction of sewers and the erection of hospitals ; he revived the industry of weaving ; and he established an academy, whose scholars spread the fame of Geneva and its influence, which was the influence of Calvin, through France and England. In these congregational, civic, and educational constructions his mind worked with power and with such freedom as may inhere in the creation of institutions.

Through the impetus of his religious convictions and the power of his constructive logic and gifts of expression, Calvin formulated an irrefragable and militant body of doctrine for the reformed church, and an accordant liturgy. Herein he built upon the work of Luther and other reformers. Though his *Christian Institute* contained little that was original with its author, it was none the less a rock of refuge and a sword of offence. In it the ardour of faith, the power and reason of conviction, lived and moved in masterful argument and words of gall and flame. A consummate book, wielding prodigious influence, moulding the minds of generations. One will find in it the plastic and expressional genius of a man refashioning the faith of Paul and Augustine and Luther.

Luther and Calvin were the protagonists of the Reformation—of the Protestant revolt from Roman Catholicism. Notwithstanding their occupation with traditional material, their intolerance of convictions other than their own, and their denial of the freedom of the will, their reinterpretation of Christianity and human life was the child of the free action of their minds. It marks a stage in the progress of intellectual freedom and civic liberty. Certain trammels of ecclesiastical and political authority were breached, although both Luther and Calvin sought to enclose within narrow and fixed barriers the Pauline freedom which they had recovered for their churches.

Moreover, their minds were not only acting with efficient freedom, but were engaged in the presentation of the best that Luther and Calvin could conceive for man. Both of these men were striving for an ideal, and straining to grasp it. They exemplify the human progress which comes through the mind's endeavour to think out what is the very best for man, and then to reach it.

In regard to Calvin and Luther, and the leaders of the religious struggle of the time which followed, one is always close to the profound problem of the effect of basic religious assurances upon human progress, and of their relation to the free action of the mind. But instead of pursuing further the interesting phenomena of this intolerant and rigid religious freedom, we may turn to philosophy for clearer illustrations of the ingenuity of the mind seeking a larger knowledge and a more universal intellectual freedom.

CHAPTER V

THE FREEDOM OF THE PHILOSOPHIC MIND

PHILOSOPHY, the quest of truth, of large, fundamental, intellectually satisfying, truth; the many ways in which this quest has turned and twisted, been baffled and apparently thrown back! Though the quest seems never to attain the goal, the knights of the spirit have not failed in their reward.

This search has been a reflection of human progress. It has also been a moving energy. What finer moving energy can there be than the conception and production of novel thoughts of general significance and possible validity? Such yield new insight and shed light on human life. If the specific opinions prove misleading, they become warning signs or fences, keeping men from falling into like pitfalls or groping along the same blind alleys. So they serve in the economy of progress. Moreover, though philosophic thoughts be austere in their expression and caviare to the vulgar, they may undergo popular transformations, and even in their corruption or misuse affect mankind. Assuredly one will set philosophy among the moving energies of human progress.

A system of philosophy, like a mode of religion or a form of art, or any branch of craft or scientific knowledge, is connected with the general conditions of the philosopher's time. One need not say that it sprang from those conditions and was but an expression of popular ideals, or a conscious buttress of accredited convictions. Yet most academically foolish is that philosopher who would seek truth mincingly, and delicately rear his tapering *flèches* above the realities of his world. As the healthy part lives and functions in the whole organism, philosophy should draw from the whole current of human life. Even though this foolish philosopher do not keep in acceptant contact with his time, we at least, as historians of philosophy and all things, must make broad the bases of our inquiry, our questing history of the interaction of the many kinds of minds in history. In our brief reflections upon the thoughts of certain salient thinkers, we will shepherd our ewe lambs with the grosser flock, and not let them stray away with upturned noses into isolated unreality.

I

THE APPROACH TO THE MODERN TIME

A few words have been said already of the Aristotelian scholasticism of the Middle Ages regarded as a free search for truth.[1] Passing on-

---

[1] *Ante*, p. 132 *sqq.*

ward, through the fifteenth and sixteenth centuries, we discern a loosening of the minds of thoughtful men from the authority of Aristotle, and a lessening of interest in the writing of the Fathers. The loosening might take the form of adopting the views of other Greek philosophers, and of acclaiming Plato as divine. Cast loose from Aristotle, men were no longer sure of their procedure : they began to act like ships at sea that are uncertain of their course.

A certain famous Nicholas of Cusa, born in 1401 and dying a cardinal in 1464, is an instance of a tireless seeker, cast amid the waters of the past, striving to choose among the eddies—think for himself. He loosed himself from Aristotle through employing the principle of *docta ignorantia*, well-taught ignorance, in order to consider afresh the limitations of human knowledge; and then broke clear away in a conception of the union of all contraries in God. But he had by no means freed his thought from scholastic conclusions, even in his physical speculations, which interested him deeply. Yet his opinion that the earth is not the centre of the universe but moves like other planets, and not in a circle, since it does not move about something fixed, was prophetic of the earth's final dethronement from its central fixity, which came in the next century. The mind of this man worked with more freedom than Aquinas had, and was beginning to evolve novel thoughts.

The century after Nicholas of Cusa saw a number of philosopher-physicists who were quite as much at sea as Nicholas, both in their metaphysics and in their physical theories, which were bold imaginings rather than inferences from observation. Telesio, Campanella, Bruno, were south Italians, who drew much trouble upon themselves for their opinions : Telesio was worried by the monks, Campanella was many years in prison, and Bruno was burned at Rome in the year sixteen hundred. Of the three, Bruno possessed the most militant temper and the most stupendous imagination. All three had flung loose from Aristotle, and despised the logic of Scholasticism. Though drawing much from the past, they felt unhampered by it. Bruno was affected by the speculations of Nicholas of Cusa, and above all had taken to himself, and flaunted as an infinite fact, the newly and timidly enunciated hypothesis of Copernicus. His imagination outsoared the solar system and the sphere of the fixed stars, and went flying through an infinite universe of endless worlds. He found the universe permeated and vivified by God, as the infinite world soul, or what you will. Bruno had freed his mind from the authority of the schools and even of the Church. However much the substance of his thought was given him, he was a free thinker with it all.

So was his contemporary, Francis Bacon. If picturesque denunciations of all previous thinking are evidence of intellectual freedom, Bacon was a free thinker among the free. The universality of his rejections rivalled those of his namesake, Roger Bacon, of the thirteenth century; and each of them was sure that he had discovered, and laid down for all time, the true method of experimental or inductive science.

In view of the defects of accepted methods and the puerility of existent knowledge, Francis Bacon saw that there was but one course for him—" to try the whole thing anew upon a better plan, and to commence a total reconstruction of sciences, arts and all human knowledge, raised upon the proper foundations." Such are his words.[1] He would not confine his aim to the " working out of some one discovery and no more, such as the nature of the magnet, the ebb and flow of the sea, the system of the heavens "; but would follow the bent of man's noblest ambition, which is " to extend the power and dominion of the human race over the Universe," an empire which " depends wholly on the arts and sciences." " All knowledge is . . . to be referred to use and action," said Francis Bacon, and constantly reiterated the same thought in various phrases. He has become famed (although Roger Bacon was before him here) as the inspirer of the beneficent utilitarian purpose of modern science.

[1] For a short discussion of Francis Bacon, see chap. xxxiv. of my *Thought and Expression in the Sixteenth Century*.

Bacon set himself to formulate an inductive method, and to accumulate a mass of facts to which the method might be applied. By following his method men would soon attain universal knowledge. But his facts were often worse than questionable, and the method, as he stated and restated and illustrated it, was never quite practicable. Yet as his writings moved men to think freely, to study nature, to experiment and hold fast to facts; as they carried vivid protests against subservience to authority and warnings against the aberrances of human reason; and as they abound in intellectual enthusiasm and proclaim the powers of the mind for the attainment of serviceable truth, their author surely is to be numbered among those who, by the free action of their minds, have advanced the progress of mankind.

II

DESCARTES

A man very different from Bacon in temper and achievement was René Descartes, who was born in Touraine in 1596 and died of pneumonia in Sweden, at the court of Queen Christina, in 1650. He was educated at a Jesuit college, where he gave himself less to study than to thinking. After a number of years of varied observation and reflection he betook himself to Holland, living in various places, as moved by his personal comfort or the convenience of his philosophic pursuits.

Every man stands on the ground, or in the swamp, of his education, his mind furnished with opinions, facts, and errors. Yet a man may be less enslaved by his education than trained by it and impelled toward the exercise of common sense. Stronger minds reconsider and prove what they have received. But only a Descartes will set himself the task of trying out his opinions from cellar to garret, or excogitating his own principles of certitude, and of applying the latter to an examination of universal science. From respect and prudence he chose not to criticize the Catholic faith in which he had been reared—cavillers suggested that he had left it by the way. Moreover, while doubtless imposing no inner restraint upon his thinking, he maintained an over-prudent reticence as to certain bristling subjects. Hearing of Galileo's condemnation, he suppressed his work entitled *Le Monde,* which set forth the revolution of the earth, and in his later *Principia Philosophiae* he sheltered himself behind a screen of intellectual tergiversation touching the same matter. He wished his books to be used in the colleges, and was anxious to exclude whatever might offend the Church or rouse the suspicions of the Jesuits, the ubiquitous instructors of youth. His precautions were vain, for his own dear Jesuits attacked him in his lifetime, and thirteen years after his death his works were put upon the Index.

He might as well have championed the cosmological truth which he cherished in his mind.

Descartes understood the physical science of his time better than Francis Bacon. He did much for optics, and devised what is now called analytical geometry. He advocated Harvey's great thesis of the circulation of the blood, and studied physiology at first hand through vivisection. In metaphysics, in mathematics, in the recognition of scientific discoveries, and the framing of physical hypotheses his mind worked with amazing energy, efficiency, and freedom. Yet the basic convictions of his abstractly reasoning intellect were metaphysical, and he made them serve as the deductive sources of physical theories. Such a mind was not to be guided by the close and persistent study of concrete fact.

All this is laid before us clearly in the famous *Discours de la méthode*, which is the autobiography of an intellect. Its author does not design to teach the method to be followed by every one who would conduct his reason aright, but only to show how " I have tried to conduct mine." Common sense or reason, by which the true is distinguished from the false, is quite evenly distributed among men. The point is to use one's faculties in the right way. He himself had the good fortune while young to find a method by which to extend his knowledge as far as the mediocrity of his intelligence would permit.

Nourished on letters from his youth, he had wished the more to follow them, since he was told that they would yield a clear and assured knowledge of everything useful in life. But he found himself embarrassed by doubts and errors, and finished these studies with a surer conviction of his ignorance. There were advantages in reading old authors and studying the science of other men. But one must beware lest, as in travelling, one become a stranger in his own land. He always loved mathematics, because of the certainty of its reasoning—but he was surprised that more had not been accomplished through it.

When years relieved him of his teachers, he set out to travel, meaning thus to search for knowledge in " le grand livre du monde,"—being still anxious to learn to distinguish the true from the false and to see before him clearly. But after sojourning in many countries he found that no assurance was to be had from observing the divers customs of men.

So he came to the decision to study within himself. He was thinking of the multifarious sources from which his opinions had been culled, many of them during the foolishness of childhood and the inexperience of youth. He determined to sweep his mind clean of them all, and permit the entry, or re-entry, only of those which levelled up with reason. He felt he must do this for himself, and for himself lay out a plan on which to conduct his life. " So like a man who walks alone and in the darkness, I resolved to move slowly and use such circumspection, that if I advanced little, at any rate I should not fall."

He might have adopted the method of logic, or have combined the methods of geometry and algebra ; but he thought a surer way lay in following sedulously four rules of his own devising :

1. To take nothing for true unless he saw that it evidently was so ; that is, never to be rash, and to include nothing in his judgements except that which presented itself so clearly and distinctly to his understanding that he could not doubt it.

2. To divide all problems into as many parts as possible.

3. To begin with the more simple and easy, and rise by degrees to the more complex.

4. To make complete enumerations and careful general reviews, so that nothing be omitted.

" The long chains of simple reasons used by geometricians to reach the most difficult demonstrations, had suggested to me that all the things that could fall within human knowledge followed each other in like manner ; and, provided one refrained from accepting anything for true which was not, and kept to the proper order in deducing one from the other, there would be nothing so remote that one might not reach it, or so hidden that one might not discover it."

Descartes speaks of applying his method first to

mathematics, and using it, or his own wits, in a simplification of algebraic notation which opened new possibilities to that science, and then of employing his method (or, again, his own wonderful mathematical insight) in the joinder of algebra to geometry, a procedure resulting in analytical geometry, which gave the old geometry the wings it sorely needed. He also drew from his method, or thought he did, rules for conducting his life, and discerning the best mode of living. Naturally, these rules confirmed him in his choice, for himself, of a life of thought.

After long reflection, he deemed he might safely employ his method to lay the metaphysical foundations of philosophy and physical science. Here, men had erred! He would reject as false his prior reasonings, and pretend that all things which ever had entered his mind had no more truth than the illusions of his dreams. But while thus determined to think all things false, he became the more assured that he who thought them false *was something*. He deemed this truth, *Je pense, donc je suis*, absolutely unshakeable by the most extravagant scepticism, and judged that he might accept it as the first principle of the philosophy that he was seeking.

It was indeed a sure foundation; but not altogether new, seeing that St. Augustine had already set it in pregnant phrases : surely we who know and love *are*; and if I am deceived, what then ? It is certain that I who am deceived exist —*si fallor, sum*. The author of the *City of God* had not built upon this foundation of certitude as daringly as Descartes would now build upon it. He had not read the old passages, but when his attention was called to the likeness between his thought and Augustine's, he gladly accepted the confirmation of the saint's authority.

He meditated further as to the nature of this being which he surely knew to exist—this *I* that was Descartes. Since thinking made the basis of his existence, he perceived that he was a *Mind*— a substance whose nature or essence consists only in thinking. This mind which was he needed no place, nor the support of any material thing; it was entirely distinct from body, more easily known. He recognized the ground of his certitude in that he saw *very clearly* that one must exist in order to think; and felt that he could abide by the general principle that the things which we conceive *very clearly and very distinctly* are true.

The difficulty lay in deciding which things are conceived distinctly. Here he was in doubt; but he saw *clearly* that it was a greater perfection to know than to doubt. So he was led to imagine a being more perfect than himself. None of the objects of the visible world seemed superior to him, but rather dependent on his nature, if they were true. He could think them all away. But a more perfect being cannot spring from one less perfect, since that would be to draw something out of nothing; and likewise he could not of himself have conceived the idea of a more perfect being, but must have received it from that being, who possessed all the perfections which he imagined; who, in a word, was God. There must be this more perfect being from whom he had derived such qualities as he, Descartes, possessed; who must also have placed in Descartes the ideas of such perfections —infinitude, omnipotence, omniscience—which he knew he lacked. Likewise he saw, very clearly as he thought, that while he could imagine triangles or material objects as existent or non-existent, he could not without contradiction conceive of God save as existent, since the most perfect being must possess existence as an attribute, just as surely as every triangle has the attribute that its three angles are equal to two right angles.

Again, Descartes had a predecessor in St. Anselm, whose writings he had not read.

So much for the metaphysical principles conceived by Descartes as pre-essential to a knowledge of the physical universe in its grander movements as well as in its special details. Metaphysics was prerequisite to the pursuit of all branches of physics and physiology. Descartes' God might be conceived as having created the universe and its laws, including man, his intellectual capacity and desire for truth; and then as consigning the universe and even man to the course and conduct of the laws of physics and to the linked and compelling power of human thinking.

M

Descartes presents his ideas regarding physical studies and the order of their pursuit in the latter part of the *Discours de la Méthode*, where he also emphasizes the practical and scientific purpose of philosophy, leading to a full command over the forces of Nature. In the preface to the French translation of his *Principia Philosophiae* he explains that " philosophy signifies the study of wisdom, and by wisdom is understood not merely prudence in affairs, but a perfect knowledge of everything that man may know, both for the conduct of his life and for the preservation of his health and the discovery of all the arts ; and in order that this knowledge should be such, it must be deduced from first causes . . . that is to say, from *principles*, which should have two essential qualities : first, they should be so clear and so evident that the human mind cannot doubt their truth, when it applies itself attentively to consider them ; and, secondly, they should be such that knowledge of other things will depend on them and cannot be had without them, but *they* may be known without any knowledge of other things. Deductions from these principles must be made in such sequence that the steps (*suite des déductions*) will be manifest."

Further on in this prefatory letter, Descartes wishes to explain the proper order of studies. He who wishes to advance beyond the vulgar stages of common knowledge should first of all form for himself a moral code to guide his actions. Next he should practise his reason in that logical method which leads to the discovery of new truth, and test his proficiency with simple problems, like those of mathematics.

" When he has acquired some facility in finding true solutions, he should apply himself in earnest to the true philosophy. Its first part, metaphysics, contains the principles of knowledge, among which is the explication of the chief attributes of God, of the immateriality of our minds (*âmes*) and of all the clear and simple notions that are in us. The second part [of philosophy] is physics, in which, having first found the true principles of material things, one examines generally the composition of the universe, then in particular, the nature of this earth and of all the bodies upon it, like air, water, fire, the loadstone and other minerals. Next there is need to examine particularly the nature of plants, of animals, and especially of man, so that one may discover other sciences useful to him.

" So all philosophy is as a tree, of which the roots are metaphysics, the trunk physics, and the branches springing from the trunk are all the other sciences, which are comprised under the chief heads of medicine, mechanics, and ethics:—I mean the highest and most perfect ethics, which, presupposing a complete knowledge of all the other sciences, is the final stage of wisdom. Yet, as one does not cull the fruit either from the roots or trunk, but only from the tips of the branches, so the chief utility of philosophy depends on those of its parts which may only be learned the last."

Calvin's intellectual clarity and power of logical presentation reappear in Descartes, a rival exemplar of the French genius. Like Calvin's theology, Descartes' philosophy consisted of clear thoughts made into a sublime structure by the force of sequential yet imaginative reasoning. Mighty is the appeal to reason in both systems, and firm the reliance on the same. And very great was the effect of each upon the contemporary world and future generations. No man ever turned more effectively from scholastic authority to human reason than Descartes in his very personally thought-out system of philosophy ; a system which sought to knit the reality of facts to the logic of ideas. To be sure, his reality was conceived with too disdainful intellectuality ; and far too sheer was his reliance on chains of deductive reasoning for the discovery of truth. But the effect of his method and of his monumental attitude was profound. " Cartesian-ism " was strengthened rather than impaired by the respectful objections of distinguished disciples. It was destined for a space to permeate the intellectual atmosphere of continental Europe. Men flouted authority more boldly, and more confidently appealed to reason, after Descartes. They also began to conceive that the problems of the physical universe might be solved through mechanical principles.

As touching our own theme in this little book, we shall not meet with a more brilliant example of the free rational working of a philosophic and mathematical mind. The laws of reasoning, which with him represent the laws of being, were the sole restraint or limit upon the freedom of his thought.

III

The Metaphysical Testing of Knowledge

Descartes and Bacon were the last great philosophers to assume that through true principles applied by the correct method men might win universal knowledge. Neither of them realized Nature's infinite complexity and exhaustless discoverability. Descartes is a supreme example of the philosophic mind working from *a priori* principles for the clarification of thought and the advancement of knowledge. He did not doubt the mind's power to know the outer world. Other men, following in close sequence, attempted to analyse cognition and test its competency. The result was a useful clipping of wings, which, however, were to grow again apace.

Foremost in this clipping was the Englishman, John Locke, who was born in 1632, eighteen years before Descartes died. The opening of his great *Essay Concerning Human Understanding* refers to the ill-success of inquiries that are carried into matters beyond human comprehension. For himself, he proposed a critical inquiry into " the origin, certainty and extent of human knowledge, together with the grounds and degrees of belief, opinion and assent." He deems it will appear that while our understanding may be inadequate to comprehend the universe, it suffices for the needs of men set upon a rational conduct of their lives.

Locke will argue that our knowledge has to do with ideas, a term which " stands best for whatsoever is the object of the understanding, when a man thinks," or " whatever it is which the mind can be employed about." Ideas make the material of our knowledge.[1] They come from " experience," that is to say, either directly from impressions upon the senses, or through a mental combination and reflection upon them. Such is the genesis and construction of all human thoughts. For the mind has no innate ideas or moulding forms in which sense-experience must be cast; no innate principles of conviction, which are neither susceptible of proof nor open to criticism.

The *Essay* passes on through close descriptions and acute discussion of mental processes. It

---

[1] " Since the mind, in all its thoughts and reasonings, hath no other immediate object but its own ideas, which it alone does or can contemplate, it is evident that our knowledge is only conversant about them. Knowledge, then, seems to me nothing but the perception of the connection and agreement or disagreement and repugnancy of any of our ideas " (*Essay, etc.*, iv., ch. i.).

exerted indelible effect upon subsequent thought, and set the intricate foundations of modern psychology.   Much of its substance seems stale because it has become part of our habitual thinking.   In his time and afterwards, however, dissatisfaction with the limitations of such pedestrian sense-philosophy incited others to further questings and devices. But Locke's dispassionate intellect had worked with freedom and ingenuity in his contribution to critical and constructive thought.

Locke merely brushed the mystery of how we know.   Others were to stir it more deeply, and first among them that very original philosophic genius, George Berkeley, who was born in 1685, and produced at the age of twenty-four his *New Theory of Vision,* intended to prepare men for his *Principles of Human Knowledge,* which appeared the following year.   If the novelty of his doctrines was repellent, the charm of his personality drew men to this dovelike and persuasive youth, whose soul was a well-spring of romance which sent him from England as far as our own Rhode Island, lured by the hope of founding a holy community of philosophers in the " remote Bermudas."   His enthusiasm and eloquent genius set men's eyes upon those far islands even as later in life he moved English society to find a panacea for bodily ills in tar-water, most harmless of decoctions, well suited to work an eighteenth - century mind - cure. Its virtues are set forth in Berkeley's remarkable prose swan-song, entitled *Siris,* which transmutes the vast material world into a sheer manifestation of the creativeness of the divine spirit and the spirits of men. Then why not tar-water ? Why might not that be a humble vehicle of fire, light, ether, the Vitalized Fire of the Universe, the intellectual plastic principle of the demiurgic and constantly remoulding Mind, which is the One that makes the All ? [1]

Thus in his old age Berkeley thought and dreamed upon philosophy. He had written in his youth : " Some truths there are so near and obvious to the mind that a man need only open his eyes to see them. Such I take this important one to be, viz. that all the choir of heaven and furniture of the earth, in a word all those bodies which compose the mighty frame of the world, have not any subsistence without a mind ; that their *being* is to be perceived or known ; [2] that consequently so long as they are not actually perceived by me, or do not exist in my mind, or that of any other created spirit, they must either have no existence at all, or else subsist in the mind of some Eternal Spirit ; it being perfectly unintelligible, and involving all the absurdity of abstraction, to attribute to any single part of them an existence independent of a spirit." [3]

[1] See *Siris : a Chain of Philosophical Reflexions and Inquiries,* §§ 285-303 and *passim.*

[2] As he elsewhere said : " Their *esse* is *percipi.*"

[3] *Principles of Human Knowledge,* § 6.

The sweep of Berkeley's lucubrations drew wings from Plato as well as from his own soul. His cosmic arguments aimed at the establishment of the world upon spirit. But in his youth Berkeley was less a scholar than a thinker; and his principles burst directly from his brain upon a misunderstanding world.

In the *New Theory of Vision*, his earliest work, he concludes " that the proper objects of vision constitute the Universal language of nature; whereby we are instructed how to regulate our actions. . . . It is by their information that we are principally guided in all the transactions and concerns of life. And the manner wherein they signify and mark out unto us the objects which are at a distance is the same with that of languages and signs of human appointment; which do not suggest the things signified by any likeness or identity of nature, but only by an habitual connexion that experience has made us to observe between them."

Thus material things are symbols, fixed in a symbolism deeper than men's arbitrary conventions. Of some conventions the young Berkeley was very sick—sick of the heavy " curtain of words " which hangs between our minds and a true vision of " the fairest tree of knowledge, whose fruit is excellent and within the reach of our hand." [1] Abstract ideas made the heaviest fold of that obscuring curtain;

[1] *Ibid.* Introd. § 24.

and Berkeley set himself to dissipate them, pouring his ridicule upon such abstract ideas as man or animal, and upon those of body, figure and magnitude, which entered into that blindest idea of all, the abstract idea of extension.[1]

This accomplished, he proceeds to argue—the very kernel of his revolutionary doctrine—that the so-called primary qualities of matter, like figure and extension, which Locke had retained as actual, have no existence apart from the perceiving mind ; for the being or *esse* of all things beyond the mind is *percipi*, that they be perceived ; and the notion of the actual existence of such qualities as great and small, swift and slow, of motion and extension, and of that monstrosity and underlying contradiction known as *matter*, " depends on that strange doctrine of abstract ideas." [2] Matter and its abstract qualities have no existence whatsoever, seeing that they are intangible, imperceptible, and inconceivable. Concrete things exist, inasmuch and in so far as they are perceived by some mind. Impressed upon human minds " according to certain rules or laws of nature, they speak themselves the effects of a Mind more powerful and wise than human spirits." These ideas have more reality than those of the imagination which the mind frames of itself apart from such impressions, even as the sun which we imagine in the stillness of the

---

[1] Introd. to *Principles*, § 7 *sqq.*
[2] *Principles*, § 9 *sqq.*

night is less real than the orb which we perceive by day.[1]

Ideas, sensations, notions, and the continual succession of ideas, which we perceive, are inactive. There must be some cause for them that must be an active incorporeal substance or spirit. It cannot lie in any bodies external to our perception; if there were such we should not know it. The ideas of sense, with their distinctness, order, steadiness, coherence, present what we call the laws of nature, and spring from the wisdom and benevolence of their author, the mind upon which we depend.

" A spirit is one simple, undivided, active being; as it perceives ideas it is called *understanding*, and as it produces or otherwise operates about them it is called the *will*. Hence there can be no idea formed of a soul or spirit; for all ideas whatever, being passive and inert, they cannot represent unto us, by way of image or likeness, that which acts." [2]

Clearly, then, such ideas as number,[3] or extension perceived in concrete forms, are but the creatures of the mind; and *time* is nothing when " abstracted from the succession of ideas in our minds." [4] These Berkeleyan principles are close to those which were to be supported by Kant's heavier reasoning. Berkeley's mind was working in freedom while it thus destroyed the objective actuality of the material

---

[1] *Principles*, § 36.   [2] *Ibid.* §§ 20-40.
[3] *Ibid.* § 12.   [4] *Ibid.* § 97.

world, and even though his argument might not be accepted as an advance toward the truth of things, men would not walk the highways of experience with the same credulity as before.

David Hume, another great predecessor and an immediate spur to Kant, had a more dissolving and less ideally constructive mind than Berkeley. He is the eighteenth-century exemplar of an extreme empiricism, that is to say, of a knowledge limited strictly for its data to experience or observation, and discarding all principles which are not evidenced by these data, and cannot be drawn from them.

Perhaps Hume's service to thought lay in bringing the ways of rational empiricism to the point where its inadequacy became evident to other minds, and indeed did not escape his own. He carries out more subtly the intellectual analysis of Locke, and accepts from Berkeley the latter's denial of abstract ideas as a great philosophical discovery, but will by no means go along with him in recognizing thought's creative and, as it were, cosmogonic virtues.

In admitting the halting and unsatisfactory nature of his own explanation of the operations of the human understanding, he felt himself thrown back upon quite unanalysable makeshifts. The first sentence in his *Treatise of Human Nature* gives his position, derived from Locke : " All the perceptions of the human mind resolve themselves into two distinct kinds, which I shall call *impressions* and *ideas*." But after many pages of acute analysis, he finds himself constrained to say :

" As to those *impressions* which arise from the senses, their ultimate cause is, in my opinion, perfectly inexplicable by human reason, and it will always be impossible to decide with certainty whether they arise immediately from the object, or are produced by the creative power of the mind, or are derived from the Author of our being." [1]

And then again, recognizing the difficulty of deciding as to the nature of " the belief of any matter of fact," he thinks that " an opinion or belief may be most accurately defined, *a lively idea related to or associated with a present impression*." But he finds that he cannot explain the difference between a belief and a fiction, save somehow in the manner of its being conceived. Belief is an *idea*, and " an idea assented to feels different from a fictitious idea, that the fancy alone presents to us." [2]

In a famous " Appendix " written long after those youthful years of analytical enthusiasm when he composed the *Treatise*, he clearly recognizes the shortcomings of his reasoning :

" Philosophers begin to be reconciled to the principle, that we have no idea of external substance distinct from the ideas of particular qualities. This must pave the way for a like principle with

---

[1] *Treatise*, I., III., V.
[2] *Treatise*, I., III., VII.

regard to the mind, that we have no notion of it, distinct from the particular perception.

" So far I seem to be attended with sufficient evidence. But having thus loosened all our particular perceptions, when I proceed to explain the principle of connection, which binds them together, and make us attribute to them a real simplicity and identity, I am sensible that my account is very defective, and that nothing but the seeming evidence of the precedent reasonings could have induced me to receive it. If perceptions are distinct existences, they form a whole only by being connected together. But no connections among distinct existences are ever discoverable by human understanding. We only *feel* a connection or determination of the thought to pass from one object to another."

So the analytic thinker is thrown back upon other and irrational tendencies of his nature, upon feeling, possibly upon fancy. " Men of bright fancies may in this respect be compared to those angels, whom the Scripture represents as covering their eyes with their wings." Yet there is danger in rejecting fancy, since " the understanding, when it acts alone . . . entirely subverts itself, and leaves not the lowest degree of evidence in any proposition, either in philosophy or common life."

Perhaps there is a refuge : when cast down by " those manifold contradictions and imperfections in human reason," then perchance " most fortunately it happens that since reason is incapable of dispelling these clouds, Nature herself suffices to that purpose, and cures me of this philosophic melancholy and delirium. . . ." [1]

Honest David Hume finds himself thrown back, incomprehensibly, upon the whole of human nature, forced to rely upon feelings which reason cannot compass or explain. But his mordant analysis had cleared philosophy of many fond futilities. Very notable is his explosion of the principle of causality, which may be supposed to have awakened Kant, as he says, from his " dogmatic slumber."

Long and penetrating, as it were from many directions, was Hume's argument against the acceptance of causation as a universal and necessary principle. He relies upon two propositions : first, " that there is nothing in any object, considered in itself, which can afford us a reason for drawing a conclusion beyond it " ; secondly, " that even after the observation of the frequent or constant conjunction of objects, we have no reason to draw any inference concerning any object beyond those of which we have had experience." [2] Hence, there is no ground for the deduction of any universal and necessary principle of causation. Elsewhere he says very clearly : " We have no other notion of cause and effect, but that of certain objects, which have been always conjoined together, and which in all

---

[1] From the concluding chapter to Book I. of the *Treatise.*
[2] *Treatise*, I., III., XII.

past instances have been found inseparable. We cannot penetrate into the reason of the conjunction. We only observe the thing itself, and always find that from the constant conjunction the objects require a union in the imagination." [1]

Locke, Berkeley, Hume, cleared away many a musty notion. Whether or not their own thought could profitably be built on, they took the wind from the sails of the grand dogmatic rationalism of Descartes, and left Spinoza standing, as it were, alone, a sheer unscalable mountain, which few men would attempt. They also evoked Kant, and led this man of strange and powerful mind to perceive the difficulties attending all knowledge ; led him to cast off his acceptances of Leibnitz's universe formed through the creative function of mind ; and pointed his intellect, his whole inquiring nature, to the problem of the mystery of mind and its cognition of outer things. [2]

Kant !—the thousands upon thousands of reams that have been devoted to this Königsberger who dwelt on the edge of the abyss of the unknowable, exploring it with his mind, dangling his plummet, knowing so much more exhaustively than other

[1] *Treatise*, I., III., VI.
[2] A remarkable and almost unknown forerunner both of Berkeley and Kant was Richard Burthogge, in his *Essay upon Reason and the Nature of Spirits*, London, 1694. See Georges Lyon, *L'Idéalisme en Angleterre en XVIII⁰ siècle*, p. 72 *sqq.* and Cassirer, *Das Erkenntnisproblem*, etc., vol. i. p. 464 *sqq.* and pp. 596-7.

men that no line could ever reach the bottom. To-day some would still find in him the necessary starting-point of philosophic thinking, while others might hold him a fatal ghostifier of thought.

He began as a Newtonian physicist and never ceased to lecture upon the physics of the cosmos— the earth and the far vaster bodies moving through the infinite heavens. And never was he unaware that, for the likes of him, physics must sound in metaphysics, in a satisfying or at least delimiting consideration of the ultimate problems of the knowing mind and its relations to the physical world. Newton was his master; Kant deemed his scientific method complete and perfect. The *Principia* was an " immortal " work, and vast was to be the knowledge and insatiate the questing of this great student of it.

Kant's earliest work, published in 1746 when he was twenty-two years old, was prophetic of his career. It was entitled " Thoughts on the true Estimate of Living Forces and Criticism of the Proofs relied upon by Leibnitz and other Mechanical Philosophers (Mechaniker) in this Controversy." The subject of the paper was a question of mathematical physics, but its wider purpose was to point out the faulty methods of physics and metaphysics, and emphasize the need of a true metaphysics for the solution of the problems of physics. An example of proper method might be seen in this paper of the young critic.

The following years brought forth his " General Natural History and Theory of the Heaven, or Essay on the Constitution and Mechanical Origin of the whole Universe (des ganzen Weltgebäudes) treated in accordance with the Principles of Newton." It was published in 1755, and the previous year there had appeared a short preliminary paper by him on the Retardation of the Rotation of the Earth. He found physical cause for this in the constant action of the tides in their movement from east to west working as a frictional force opposing the earth's rotation from west to east. This discovery attracted little attention for a century, but has been accredited to Kant in our time.[1]

The *Natural History of the Heavens* unfolded the towering ambitions of the youth who attacked the mathematics of Descartes and Leibnitz at the age of twenty-two. It proceeded from the basis of the Newtonian physics, proving the mutual attraction of bodies ; to which should be added the counter impulse of repulsion as exhibited, for example, in the movements of vapours. It accepted the matter of the world as in a state of chaos or general dispersion at the beginning—further back it would

[1] See the Introduction to W. Hastie's *Kant's Cosmogony*, which gives a full translation of this Essay and of Kant's far larger *Natural History, etc., of the Heavens* (Glasgow, 1900). For Kant's works on physics, the reader may be referred to this book and to Konrad Dieterich, *Die Kant'sche Philosophie in ihrer inneren Entwicklungsgeschichte* (being a second edition of the same writer's *Kant und Rousseau*, 1885).

not go! Newton had accounted for the present
movements of at least the solar system. Kant
sought to describe the process through which arose
the movements and general constitution of the solar
system and all the constellations of the heavens.
If Newton set forth the laws by which this universe
subsists, Kant would set forth those through which
it arose. He is convinced that whatever applies
to the solar system holds throughout the universe.

The result at which he arrived has since been
termed the Nebular Hypothesis. For many years
Kant's great speculation slept rather resignedly in
his little-known work, till, with sundry modifications and a better equipment of argument, a like
hypothesis was set forth by Laplace.[1] Kant's own
argumentation had been large, and his vision of the
physical universe sublime. The reader is carried
out into the universe, with " its immeasurable
greatness, and infinite variety and beauty, filling
us with wonder." Kant views its star-systems as
" members in the chain of the totality of nature,"
and subject to eventual disintegration and dispersal,
even as through untold millions of years they have
reached their present forms. " Newton, that great
admirer of the attributes of God from the perfection
of His works, who combined with the deepest insight
into the excellence of nature the greatest reverence
for the Divine Omnipotence, saw himself compelled

[1] For instance, in the closing chapters, and final note, to
his *Système du Monde.*

to predict the decay of nature by the natural tendency of the mechanics of motion. If a Systematic Constitution, by the inherent consequence of its perishableness through great periods brings even the very smallest part nigh to the state of disorder, there must be a moment at which this gradual diminution will have exhausted all motion."

Nature is infinitely prodigal. The destruction of worlds is a shadow amid her innumerable suns. So great is the infinitude of creation that a Milky Way of worlds is to it as a flower or insect to our earth. Kant's vision at the last becomes apocalyptic, as it descries the divine plan and the immortal soul of man—happy soul if amid the tumult of the elements she may see as from an unshaken height the devastation of things perishable, and find true fellowship with the Infinite Being.[1]

This far reasoner upon the mechanism of the origin, subsistence, and decay of the universe is willing to accept the imagined reproach to his audacity, in that he seemed to say, " Give me matter and I will show you how a world shall arise out of it." Yet, however reliant upon the arguments of the Newtonian physics, he senses his ignorance of biological science, which was not yet. Spheres and their orbits may be referred to simple mechanical causes. But as to plants or insects, we cannot say : " Give me matter and I will show you

---

[1] *Natural History of the Heavens*, chap. vii. The quotations are from Hastie's translation, slightly modified.

how a caterpillar can be produced." Indeed, " the
formation of all the heavenly bodies, the cause of
their movements, and, in short, the origin of the
whole present constitution of the universe, will
become intelligible before the production of a single
herb or a caterpillar by mechanical causes will be
understood." [1]

So wrote Kant, before 1755, when this work was
published and its author was thirty-one years old.
Though he now qualified as lecturer at the Königs-
berg University, he did not receive his appointment
to the chair of philosophy till fifteen years later.
Physics never ceased to occupy him, and he lectured
upon Physical Geography to the end of his career,
with an ever larger knowledge of mathematical and
physical science. Equally keen had been his interest in the metaphysical problems of the knowing
mind, and he had always been seeking to establish
and correlate these two domains of thought, physics
and metaphysics, and assure the foundations of the
former in the latter. In the decade preceding 1781,
when he published the *Critique of Pure Reason*, he
gave himself over to the basic satisfaction of his
mind in the solution of the fundamental problem
of knowledge—How do we know? How, as he
phrases it, are synthetic judgements *a priori* possible?
In this great physicist's eventual devotion to metaphysics one recognizes an impulse analogous to that
which had pushed Greek philosophy on from the

---

[1] *Natural History of the Heavens*, Introduction.

physical hypotheses of Thales and his successors to a more fundamental examination of the nature and consistency of human knowledge.

Matter, force, causality, the rational unity of the universe, including mankind and its history, were problems pressing on his mind ; and the establishment of rational conceptions of space and time and movement, and the metaphysical problems of the mind itself, and its experience and knowledge. The value of his consideration of these subjects is still ardently upheld and violently contested. Possibly no man before him, or since his day, so profoundly examined the limitations of the mind. Did his metaphysics mark the unavoidable lines of all further thinking and intellectual progress ? Few are in the mood to-day to maintain this. clarification might issue from the realization of the futility of such reasonings, and perhaps a warning to follow other paths.

Kant says himself that it was Hume's attack upon the necessity and universality of the principle of cause and effect that first awakened him from his " dogmatic slumber," [1] meaning by this phrase, " the dogmatic procedure of reason without any previous criticism of its own powers." This was the weakness of all previous metaphysics, laying it open to the attacks of scepticism. The object of his great work, the *Critique of Pure Reason*, was to

---

[1] Introduction to the *Prolegomena*, published in 1783, two years after the *Critique of Pure Reason*.

supply a criticism of metaphysic, to wit, a criticism of the faculty of reason in so far as it seeks *a priori* knowledge, which is independent of experience.

All knowledge begins with experience, but may not originate from it. For experience is made up of sense-impressions, but apparently with another element which the understanding or faculty of knowing supplies upon the occasion of these impressions. That element of knowledge is said to be *a priori*, to distinguish it from empirical knowledge, which comes *a posteriori, i.e.* from experience. *A priori* knowledge is characterized by its necessity and universality, qualities which experience cannot supply. Mathematical propositions afford instances of it, and so does the principle that there can be no change without a cause.

A science like mathematics may advance *a priori* without the aid of experience. But neither mathematics nor any form of *a priori* knowledge can advance by sheer analysis of conceptions already possessed. There can be no advance through analytic predications or judgements, but only through *synthetic* judgements, which are not mere identical propositions, but amplify the subject, by adding in the predicate something not necessarily implied in the subject. Judgements from experience are always synthetic, adding something to the subject. Pure *a priori* judgements draw nothing from experience, and yet may, as in mathematics, be synthetic. The proposition that the sum of the angles of a triangle is equal to two right angles adds to our knowledge of triangles, and yet is established by reason and not from experience. Likewise the science of physics rests on synthetic *a priori* judgements, as, for example, that throughout all changes in the material world the quantity of matter remains the same.

As for metaphysics, its problem, the problem of pure reason, is to show how *a priori* synthetic judgements are possible ; how it is that, without drawing from experience, the predicate can enrich our conception or knowledge of the subject, which, Kant says, is a matter of transcendental knowledge.

The massive *Critique of Pure Reason* consists of the solution of this problem. This book, as all men know, or at least have been told, proceeds through an argumentation of absorbing interest for those who are able to follow it. It begins with an analysis of space and time, the two pure forms of sensible perception, which constitute principles of *a priori* knowledge. All our experience of the outer world is limited to an experience of the linked impressions of phenomena coming to us under the *a priori* principles of their perception in space and time. The outer world is thus empirically real and transcendentally ideal.

From these transcendental principles of sensible perception, Kant passes to the universal rules of the understanding, which he calls Transcendental Logic. That portion which sets forth the pure

element of knowledge belonging to the understanding and the principles without which no
object can be thought, is termed Transcendental
Analytic. Through the spontaneous action of the
understanding, the complex content of perception
is taken up in thought and combined into the unity
of consciousness. This combination or synthesis
is threefold, consisting first in the apprehension in
perception of various ideas or mental modifications ;
next in their reproduction in imagination ; and,
thirdly, their recognition in conception. The unity
of consciousness, which is a consciousness of personal identity, is prior to all data of perception, and
gathers up all possible phenomena of an individual's
experience.

" *I think* " must be capable of accompanying
all my ideas. It is a spontaneous act, not due
to sense. Therefore it is pure, not empirical,
apperception, and sounds in my self-consciousness.
All combination is the work of understanding,
which indeed is the faculty of combining *a priori*,
and bringing under the unity of apperception the
various determinations given in perception.

The human understanding is cognitive and
regulative through its *a priori* principles of perception in space and time, and the equally *a priori*
categories or pure conceptions of the understanding.
These do not hang upon the caprice of any individual. They are universal and necessary forms
of thought, and as such prescribe laws to the

phenomena of Nature when the latter are perceived. Since these phenomena have no existence apart from the perceiving subject, so they have no laws save those set by his understanding in transforming them into knowledge in accordance with its universal spontaneities or forms of thinking. The necessity and universality of these forms prevent the subject from perceiving phenomena in any unrelated and arbitrary fashion, and imbue the phenomena of Nature with the universal and objective laws of the forms of thought in accord with which all human understanding cannot but know and understand and reason.

These few inadequate sentences may give some dubious notion of Kant's Transcendental Analytic. We shall not enter the mazes of Transcendental Dialectic in which he tracks the illusions of the understanding, and exposes the fallaciousness of the reasoning processes that pass beyond all relationship with the phenomena of experience. Such are the reasonings which strive to prove the existence of God, the substantiality and immortality of the soul, and the freedom of the human will. These matters are beyond the powers of reason, and yet we are irresistibly driven to their consideration, even to their acceptance as truths. " Therefore I have found it necessary," says Kant in his Preface, " to deny *knowledge* of God, freedom, and immortality, in order to find a place for *faith*."

In other treatises, by other modes of argument

—for it still is argument—Kant seeks to establish these truths and lodestars of man's moral life. Perhaps his arguments here have been found no more convincing than those of other men. The *Metaphysic of Morality*, with its noble principles, is the most impressive.

"There is nothing conceivable in the world or indeed outside of it, that can be held good without qualification, except a good will."

"A man's will is good, not because the consequences flowing from it are good, nor because it is able to attain the end it seeks; it is good in itself, or because it wills the good," a statement to hold fast to in these days of dissolute opportunism and pragmatism. Note the next sentence: "By a good will is not meant mere well-wishing; it consists in a resolute employment of all the means within one's reach, and its intrinsic value is in no way increased by success or lessened by failure." This recalls Luther's robust separation of veritable working faith from mere belief.

Reason is a sorry means of gaining happiness; which implies "that life has another and nobler end than happiness, and the true vocation of reason is to secure that end."

"Duty is the obligation to act from reverence for law." Kant was a good Prussian.

"I must act in such a way that at the same time I can will that my rule of conduct should become a universal law."

Moral " imperatives are expressed by the word *ought* to indicate that the will upon which they are binding is not necessarily determined to conformity with the objective law of reason. If the action is conceived as good in itself, the imperative is categorical."

Every man is an end in himself and not merely a means to be used. Then " act so as to use humanity, whether in your own or in another's person, always as an end, never as merely a means."

" The will is the causality of living beings in so far as they are rational. Freedom is that causality in so far as it can be regarded as efficient without being determined to activity by any cause other than itself. Natural necessity is the property of all non-rational beings to be determined to activity by some cause external to themselves." [1]

Philosophy and metaphysics are the systematic functional expression of the desire for ultimate truth, and represent the human mind freely searching for it. That they are not merely an exponent but a factor in human progress may be illustrated from the philosophers we have just been speaking of. Recall Hume's criticism of the *a priori* principle of causation, together with Berkeley's doctrine as to time and space and Kant's metaphysics touching these two postulates. The searchlight of recent mathematical physics is thrown upon the same

[1] I have used to advantage Prof. Watson's *Selections from Kant*, and taken from it some of my extracts.

problems ; and it appears that these philosophers were wending their way to positions metaphysically analogous to those at which mathematicians and physicists seem to be arriving by other paths. Philosophers and scientists appear to agree in holding that time and space are not self-existent, but dependent on events : with Kant on the events of one's mind, with the modern scientist upon events conceived as existing outside of it. Our scientists have not been unaffected by the troubles of their metaphysical predecessors.

Kant closes my illustrations of what seems to me the free action of the human mind searching for truth through sheer philosophy or metaphysics. We turn to the ways of science.

CHAPTER VI

THE SCIENTIFIC MIND

MATTERS belonging to different provinces of intellectual achievement are often designated by a single word, for convenience or perhaps from lack of perception. Such a word is Art;[1] and such another word is Philosophy, which covers the speculations, even the best resolves, of the meditative human self. Philosophy is no single topic. One might write a volume on the varied meanings of the term.

Provisionally, with some vagueness and confusion, " science " is distinguished from those supposed *a priori* deductions, and corresponding universal or necessitated mental processes, grouped under the head of philosophy or dubbed metaphysics. Accepting, likewise vaguely and provisionally, this separation of science from philosophy, we hasten to observe that science also is one of those words which cover much that is diverse. Science, the direct, systematic and rational investigation of nature, has followed many ways

---

[1] See *post*, p. 272, note.

190

into many fields, and has been led by many motives. Though one should conceive a formula broad enough to hold the basic method or rationale of all scientific procedure, nevertheless, the faces and surfaces of actual scientific processes would differ. The way of mathematics, and of mathematical physics, show slight apparent kinship with the dissections of Vesalius or Harvey, or the keen microscopy of the modern cytologist.

The rudiments lie in common observation and the practice of the crafts. Science arises from the more systematic and purposeful investigation of the data of experience ; from grouping them after their apparent relations, and from considering the how and why of their occurrence. It is an endeavour to rationalize observed phenomena and " simplify " them. And since mankind is social and articulate, the beginning and likewise the progress of the scientific consideration of the world carry the impulse to state the results, and to communicate and transmit them.

As for the scientific method there are shades of difference due to the subject - matter and the intellectual temper of the individual scientist. But the testimony of the senses and a reliance upon experience, somehow tested, compared, and logically adjusted, are the foundation. The method of the scientist lies also in his choice of facts, his choice of significant, constantly recurring, rather than meaningless sporadic facts ; the facts which most readily lend themselves to generalization or simplification in a descriptive statement, which is the statement of a law.

As, of course, every investigator in his choice of facts and the invention of experiments through which to shape and clarify his experience, proceeds on some working hypothesis; otherwise his facts are but an haphazard collection, having no interrelation, and not lending themselves to classification, generalization, and simplification—which is always the end in view. But the investigator should beware of what Henri Poincaré calls " unconscious hypotheses," which as of course will enter, and perhaps vitiate, his work, since they are part of his personal or scientific equation. They are his prepossessions, from which no man is altogether free. Prepossessions, indeed, are the bygone attainments of the mind. They represent the latent experience lying behind every conscious intellectual attitude. They form the stage from which the scientist views the field of his investigation. But he should realize the nature of the ground on which he stands.

The fields of investigation were always multifarious, and have multiplied in the recent centuries. And how different have been the motives of investigators! With the old Greeks (who had leisure) the quest of knowledge was aristocratic, largely for the sake of knowing, and usually without the thought of gain or the wish to benefit mankind.

Modern science is more commonly impelled or directed in its researches by the desire to master Nature by understanding her, and often has social, material, economic betterment for its aim. It would prove itself useful, is philanthropic, benevolent, or industrial, seeking material results and even gross rewards. It has not the detachment of Greek science.[1]

The usefulness and profit of scientific investigations in the last two centuries have strengthened enormously the thews and sinews of research and enlisted thousands in scientific labour. The utility of " applied " science has been a great factor in modern scientific progress. Nevertheless, certainly in the past and probably to-day, the curiosity of gifted men holds a leading rôle in the progress of natural science, as it has held in philosophy and in every field of human knowledge and reflection. An end is more apt to be reached when directly sought with singleness of motive. Those who have pursued the end of knowing have done more to increase human knowledge, including natural science, than those who have pursued the end of doing. There has been, moreover, the clearest intellectual freedom in the endeavours of those who simply sought to know.

[1] Yet our best scientists follow knowledge for its own sake, and investigate for the sake of the investigation. Said Simon Newcomb : " The true man of science has no such expression in his vocabulary as ' useful knowledge.' "

I

THE WAY OF GREEK SCIENCE

In the way of method, Greek science, compared with modern investigation, practised a minimum of systematic observation and experiment with a maximum of general or theoretical reasoning. The Greeks disliked drudgery, and some of their philosophers loved to think that observation and experiment made the lower part ; the better part was reasoning, perhaps from the results of observation or with its results in mind. The fruits of reason were more perfect and beautiful, less subject to error than the observations and experiments of the senses. Very extreme is the expression of Socrates in Plato's *Republic* : " Since this fretted sky is still a part of the visible world, we are bound to regard it, though the most beautiful and perfect of visible things, as far inferior nevertheless to those true revolutions which real velocity and real slowness, existing in true number and in all true forms, accomplish relatively to each other . . . which are verily apprehensible by reason and thought, but not by sight. . . . Therefore, we must employ that fretted sky as a pattern or plan to forward the study which aims at those higher objects." [1]

[1] *Republic*, 529, Davies and Vaughan's translation. Modern mathematical physics need not be unsympathetic toward this passage.

Distinctive methods would develop in Greek science and philosophy as intellectual aims diverged and the objects of inquiry were diversified. The first general result had been a mammoth rational guess, an hypothesis suggested by observation, as to the origin of the world of visible things. That water was the source of all things, or undifferentiated matter, or the moist air through condensation, each of these hypotheses was at least a substitute for mythology, and had behind it some consideration of natural processes.[1]   These beginners also observed the stars, and reflected upon the mechanics of familiar things. They were geometricians. With them geometry became a chosen province of the mind and a source of rational and constraining principles applying to the movements of the heavens and to all things on the earth.   The mathematically reasoning sciences, geometry, astronomy, physics, were to be typically Greek.   But the Greeks were also to investigate living organisms closely and even

[1] " Matter, in its modern scientific sense, is a return to the Ionian effort to find in space and time some stuff which composes nature.   It has a more refined signification than the early guesses at earth and water by reason of a certain vague association with the Aristotelian idea of substance. Earth, water, air, fire, and matter, and finally ether, are related in direct succession so far as concerns their postulated characters of ultimate substrata of nature.   They bear witness to the undying vitality of Greek philosophy in its search for the ultimate entities which are the factors of the fact disclosed in sense-awareness.   This search is the origin of science " (A. N. Whitehead, *The Concept of Nature*, p. 19 (Cambridge, 1920)).

experimentally.   Aristotle was one of the supreme zoologists of all time.

Thus Greek science began with consideration of the obvious frame and modes of things.   It was an inquiry into the *why* and *how*—a very closely related, if dual, inquiry.   The *why* pushes the inquirer one step back ; so does the *how* impel him to look behind the thing or process to some more fully explanatory or unfolding antecedent.

As touching the general problem of the world's origin, the *how* and *why* might naturally run into each other.   It was here that the Greek mind, pushed back and back, took to considering the *rationale* of matter and material things.   It fell among the thorns of more than one logical dilemma, and was driven to exercise itself on general principles and deductions, hypotheses of the intellect, which should be more irrefragable, more absolute than any conclusion from clashing observations.   Thought itself must erect the constraining universal principle or truth, the pattern to which sensible things must conform.

With Heraclitus, with Parmenides and Plato, thought passed behind or beyond observation, and found within itself constructive principles of truth and reality.   This going behind physics is metaphysics.   The metaphysician or philosopher may be interested in applying his theories to the visible world ; but his constructive principles are drawn from thought, rather than observation, and will mould to their abstract and perfectly functioning patterns all things tangible or visible.[1]

While Greek natural philosophy was changing to metaphysics, specific provinces of natural inquiry separated themselves out from it, and made manifest their objects and their method. Yet there was to be no definite separation between Greek philosophy and Greek natural science. Greek science was apt to lean against philosophy, and loved to shape its results to the dictates of the philosophic reason. There was a mighty bond between them in the conviction, which they shared, that order and law reigned throughout the world of nature as surely as just and retributive fate reigned in the world of men. The order of nature was as just as the fate which punished human crime. This was the faith of Greek philosophy, of Greek science, and of Greek religion. It held together the world of man and nature and made it one.

II

The Modern Era
Mathematics and the Physical Sciences

Because of the characteristics of Greek science

---

[1] Of this, two thousand years after Plato, Descartes affords a perfect illustration. His constructive principles were metaphysical, and while he interested himself with physics, he conformed the visible world to the constraining patterns of his *a priori* thinking. He was a metaphysician or philosopher, if one will use that term, and not a scientist.

and the comparatively limited scope of the Greek scientific achievement, we may draw from modern science ampler and clearer illustration of the freedom and energy of the human mind, reaching after knowledge and power through methodical observation, hypothesis, and experimental testing.   Modern science rises, say in the fifteenth and sixteenth centuries, partly from the supports of ancient doctrine, but for the most part from observation. Through new or reinvigorated tests of observation and then experiment, it will criticize and partially reject the old conclusions.   It will enlarge its scope and find new provinces.   Through more penetrating observation, through rationalized and more probable hypotheses, through a novel mathematics and the enlightenment of ingenious and pertinent experiment, it will advance from knowledge to further knowledge, from conclusion to conclusion, and from strength to strength, gaining the knowledge which is power over that which is known. Constantly it has encountered the opposition of superstition and authoritative false opinion, and also has had to cast off many a darling prepossession of its own.   In spite of occasional enlightening reversals, it has steadily enlarged its dominion and established its acceptance among men, and has become masterful in its dictates.   Triumph upon triumph seem to await its still youthful energies, though to-day its future, with the future of all our civilization, is threatened by an emboldened and aggressive ignorance, whose marplot passions may replace the old ecclesiastic intolerance of the free advance of truth.

Besides this sinister portent, the recent progress of science has not been smooth. Physics and mechanics, since the close of the last century, have been passing through a revolution of their own : and the end is not in sight. A multitude of novel facts have come to light, which so far have not been ordered in certain and accepted systems. The axioms and basic conceptions of these two sciences seem shaken ; and inasmuch as they are themselves fundamental, and affect, if they do not constitute, the bases of other physical sciences, many funda-mental scientific concepts are again called up for re-examination. Probably much that seemed as-sured thirty years ago will be modified. Yet this stirring of the scientific depths is of good omen, and all the more buoyantly science presses forward in the hope of a broader and surer re-establishment of truth.

Since there will be much to say of the frequent modifications of scientific opinion, it is well always to bear in mind the sure advance of tested know-ledge in strong and eager periods of history, among which we certainly may include our own time. The brilliant Greek achievement in science was followed by a lengthy diversion of human interest into other channels. But this in turn was suc-ceeded by the grand expansion of physical inquiry coming in the sixteenth century, or before, and pressing on in ever mightier volume to the present day. If we keep before our eyes the story of this triumphant effort, we shall not be confused by recent discoveries, which seem to bring reversals of previous conclusions. Rather, we shall recognize that it is the power of the present intellectual effort which seems to shake the bases of scientific knowledge while actually strengthening and enlarging them.

Quantity and number and relationship are universal elements of phenomena. With the moderns, as previously with the Greeks, arithmetic and geometry were destined to become the sciences of numerical and quantitative relationship, and the rational mode of its expression. Algebra (unknown to the Greeks) is the generalization and extension of arithmetic,[1] and analytical or " algebraical " geometry (devised by Descartes) will be the application of algebraic, that is, symbolically generalized, equations to those spacial relationships which make the province of geometry. More inclusively, mathematics, of which the above are elementary branches, may be regarded as the science of exact relationships among quantities or magnitudes or actions, and the comprehensive method of certain deduction of unknown from

---

[1] " Algebra is devised to keep the facts in abeyance while we dispassionately examine their relations " (Mark Barr).

known quantities.[1] This conception may be further generalized, and mathematics will become the science concerned with logical deductions, the drawing of necessary consequences.

The principles of mathematics seem to form part of all scientific reasoning and formulation. Its methods and results have been regarded as definite and certain, as readily proved, or tested for possible error. It still offers itself as a model for the other sciences, or at least as the ideal toward which they well may strain.

Thus mathematics, if not the model of all scientific reasoning, at least indicates the method by which

---

[1] Perhaps this sentence represents an antiquated view. Says Bertrand Russell : " In former days it was supposed (and philosophers are still apt to suppose) that quantity was the fundamental notion of mathematics. But nowadays, quantity is banished altogether, except from one little corner of geometry, while order more and more reigns supreme. The investigation of different kinds of series and their relations is now a very large part of mathematics, and it has been found that this investigation can be conducted without any reference to quantity, and, for the most part, without any reference to number " (from *Mathematics and the Metaphysicians*).
Less paradoxically, in a lecture given at King's College, London, in 1921, Prof. J. W. Nicholson says that mathematics has for its subject " a class of subjects of very different types, connected only by the one dominating characteristic of being logical accounts of some set of conceptions or of phenomena which can be stated in quantitative, and not merely general or qualitative terms " ; and he says he would " like to define Mathematics as Quantitative Science, either of the present or perhaps of the future—excluding the actual registering of a formula which describes a phenomenon, but including any logical deduction of that formula from a general principle."

the mind may apply itself with assurance to the computation and ordering of the results of its experience or observation. Mathematics is not so obviously a method or tool of observation, nor a channel through which the experience of the outer world may pass to the observer's mind. Its processes apply rather to the computation and adjustment, the rationalizing indeed, of observed phenomena. It has no concrete content of its own. Itself abstract, the content must be furnished from the observations or fund of concrete knowledge belonging to the science to which its method is to be applied.

Clearly, mathematics may be more efficiently and comprehensively applied to some sciences than to others. With some it is not only the mode of reasoning, but becomes a constructive method of investigation. Such are the sciences of mechanics and astronomy, which are especially mathematical. The data of mechanics, if not simple, largely belong to the common observation of mankind. The movements of bodies may be observed, and the facts tested by observation, as when Galileo showed that large bodies did not fall faster than small ones. Indeed all the laws which govern or, more exactly speaking, describe the facts of mechanics or astronomy are tested through their correspondence with common experience or by purposeful experiment or observation. Yet these so-called laws of the movements of bodies on the earth, and of the

earth itself and all the heavenly bodies, are calculated and constructed only through mathematics,
and formulated in mathematical terms. So worked
the Greek astronomers and Archimedes of Syracuse,
and so worked Copernicus and Galileo; and so
works Einstein. Indeed the movements of the
heavenly bodies have been found so intricate and
obscure, that they can be described or expressed
only through the abbreviated and efficient symbolism
of the higher mathematics. This is quite true,
though the results must be confirmed by visual
observation through the telescope. So mathematics furnishes the only language which physics,
including celestial and terrestrial mechanics, can use.

On the other hand, the biological sciences are
not patently mathematical either in the statement
of their formulae or the testing of their results.
Nevertheless some of their votaries use mathematics
effectively, and may set before themselves an ideal
of eventual mathematical formulation, springing
perhaps from the growing realization of the intimate connection between all physical sciences, and
the impossibility of their delimitation one from
another.

The modern scientific attitude is first made clear
in the expressions of that universal inaugurator of
modern science and its methods, Leonardo da Vinci.
His motto is observation, investigation, experiment,
all embraced under the term experience, *esperienza*
the *maestra vera.* " Those sciences are vain and

full of errors, which are not born of *esperienza*, mother of all certitude, and which do not terminate in experience cognized, that is, whose origin or middle or end comes through none of the five senses." [1]

But the treatment of the contents of this experience must be mathematical: "No human inquiry can be called true science, unless it proceeds through mathematical demonstrations." They alone bring certitude to the final test. Nature's forces are quantitative, *i.e.* mathematical. "The bird is a machine working through mathematical law." The true investigator will first observe and experiment, set forth the facts, and then demonstrate by reason why they are constrained to work as they do.

So far Leonardo, most observant of painters, and a universal genius, entranced with the investigation of the laws, the *infinite ragioni*, of the visible world of nature. He was drawn as keenly by physics and engineering as by human anatomy and physiology and the aspects and functions of plants. Though the contents of his manuscripts may have had little direct effect upon the course of science after him, still, as it were, out from the activities of his universal scientific curiosity the various branches of modern science seem to unfold.

First we note those sciences for which mathe-

---

[1] Yet Roger Bacon had said that arguments do not make us certain until confirmed by experimental tests. See *The Mediaeval Mind*, ii. p. 532 (2nd and 3rd editions).

matics supplies the method and tool of investigation, although the veritable data are furnished by observation. Early in the fifteenth century the fertile-minded Nicholas of Cusa declared that the earth moved like the planets, and somewhat later Leonardo agreed with him that the earth was not the fixed centre of the universe. The sun rather was the central body. Copernicus was twenty-one years younger than Leonardo, and though of northern birth, studied mathematics and astronomy in Italy. His awakened insight led him to reject the old explanations of the movements of the heavenly bodies, and to turn to the contrary hypothesis of the rotation of the earth upon its axis, and its revolution around the sun. Thereafter he spent his life observing the heavenly bodies, studying the recorded observations of the ancients, and devoting his genius to the mathematical calculations which should reduce the data of these observations to general principles substantiating his hypothesis. His great *De Revolutionibus* was finally printed and brought to him as he lay unconscious on his death-bed in the year 1543.

His work was far from perfect. He had retained in his calculations certain mathematical devices of Greek astronomers which only seemingly corresponded with the observed movements of the planets ; and his hypothesis erroneously assumed that the earth and other planets revolved in circles. Its credibility was impaired by the faulty conceptions prevailing in physics. Keppler discarded the old mathematical devices, and set himself to prove through further calculations that the planets moved in ellipses around the sun, with the latter at one focus of the ellipse. His mathematical imagination drove him on to describe the quantitative relations, in time as well as in space, of the movements of the solar system, till he reached their correct mathematical formulae. Galileo discovered the valid laws of mechanics which cleared away the mechanical obstacles to the acceptance of the Copernican hypothesis. He also showed it in operation by disclosing with his telescope the satellites of Jupiter revolving around their planet.

These two men were born in the generation following the death of Copernicus. Galileo, outliving Keppler, died in 1642, the year of Newton's birth, who was destined to rationalize these conceptions of the solar system in his grand generalization of the law, or fact, of gravitation.

The achievements of Galileo or Newton illustrate their scientific method better than their concise and rather casual statements describe it. The greatest scientific discoverers usually have had least to say about method, doubtless realizing that it is a simple affair quite overtopped by the genius of the investigator. One might follow Galileo's method in his discoveries and proofs of the laws of motion as finally put together in those dialogued " Discourses and Mathematical Demonstrations concerning Two

New Sciences." [1] The latter of these two sciences, which treats of motion and demonstrates its laws geometrically, was in fact and truth the creation of this mighty physicist. Lagrange said a hundred years later that *La Dynamique*, the science of accelerative and retarding forces and the movements resulting, is entirely the work of the moderns, and Galileo founded it.

" My purpose," says Galileo at the beginning of the Third Day's Dialogue, " is to set forth a new science dealing with a very ancient subject. There is in nature perhaps nothing older than motion. . . . I have *discovered by experiment* some properties of it which are worth knowing and which have not hitherto been either *observed* or *demonstrated*."

Pregnant suggestions of his manner ! Certain propositions concerning uniform motion having first been demonstrated, the discussion passes to accelerated motion. It will not concern itself with imaginary motions, but solely with " the phenomena of bodies falling with an acceleration such as actually occurs in nature," and Galileo will make his definition or description " of accelerated motion exhibit the essential features of observed accelerated motions." He believes he has been successful, and is confirmed in this belief " mainly by the consideration that experimental results are seen to agree with . . .

[1] English translation by Crew and De Salvio : *Dialogues concerning Two New Sciences* (Macmillan Co., 1914), from which my extracts are taken.

those properties which have been, one after another, demonstrated by us.   Finally, in the investigation of naturally accelerated motion we were led, by the hand as it were, in following the habit and custom of nature herself . . . to employ only those means which are most common, simple, and easy."

One pauses to note Galileo's predilection for the idea that Nature will follow the simplest possible way and employ the simplest means.[1]   He continues : " For I think no one believes that swimming or flying can be accomplished in a manner simpler or easier than that instinctively employed by fishes and birds."

" When, therefore, I observe a stone initially at rest falling from an elevated position and continually acquiring new increments of speed, why should I not believe that such increases take place in a manner which is exceedingly simple ? . . . If now we examine the matter carefully, we find no addition or increment more simple than that which repeats itself always in the same manner.   This we readily understand when we consider the intimate

---

[1] Modern science holds no such opinion : " I agree that the view of Nature which I have maintained in these lectures is not a simple one.   Nature appears as a complex system whose factors are dimly discerned by us.   But is not this the very truth ? . . . the aim of science is to seek the simplest explanations of complex facts.   We are apt to fall into the error of thinking that the facts are simple because simplicity is the goal of our quest.   The guiding motto in the life of every natural philosopher should be, Seek simplicity and distrust it " (Whitehead, *The Concept of Nature*, p. 168).

relationship between time and motion; for just as . . . we call a motion uniform when equal distances are traversed during equal time intervals, so we may . . . picture to our mind a motion as uniformly and continuously accelerated when, during any equal intervals of time whatever, equal increments of speed are given to it. Thus, if any equal intervals of time whatever have elapsed, counting from the time at which the moving body left its position of rest and began to descend, the amount of speed acquired during the first two time-intervals will be double that acquired during the first time-interval alone; so the amount added during three of these time-intervals will be treble; and that in four, quadruple that of the first time-interval. . . ." [1]

Further on, the chief speaker in the Dialogue puts aside the suggested discussion of the *cause* of the acceleration of freely falling bodies. Here as elsewhere, Galileo is intent upon true descriptions and correct formulas for the movements of naturally accelerated bodies, and declines to discuss *why* they act as they do. His purpose at present is " merely to investigate and to demonstrate some of the properties of accelerated motion, whatever the cause

[1] " Galileo felt sure that Nature would choose the simplest way. He did not realize that he was centred upon the mind's easiest way and that the real simplicity (for us, in the end) is that of an interconnected invariance in description " (Mark Barr). For " the simplest way " later thinking may have substituted the possibly analogous idea of " the line of least resistance."

P

of this acceleration may be, meaning thereby a motion such that the momentum of its velocity goes on increasing after departure from rest, in simple proportionality to the time, which is the same as saying that in equal time-intervals the body receives equal increments of velocity," and if these properties, as they will be demonstrated later, are found to be realized in freely falling and accelerated bodies, we may conclude that our definition covers their motion, and that their speed increases in the same ratio as the time and duration of the motion.

Thus one may observe Galileo outlining and preparing to follow his method of actual observation and experiment and geometrical demonstration. In the remainder of the Dialogue he advances, theorem by theorem, pausing at convenient moments to describe the experiments which showed the actual correspondence of the facts of bodies freely falling, or rolling down inclined planes, with his definition of accelerated motion and his demonstration of its properties. Afterwards he passes to the investigation of the more complex motions of projectiles in parabolic curves, which he was the first to demonstrate. This is the theorem which will be proved : " A projectile, which is carried by a uniform horizontal motion compounded with a naturally accelerated vertical motion, describes a path which is a semi-parabola."

Casually he states his scientific method as he is passing from a certain proposition shown to be most probable, but not yet proved : " Let us then, for the present, take this as a postulate, the absolute truth of which will be established when we find that the inferences from it correspond to and agree perfectly with experiment."

With Newton likewise the sureness and sufficiency of his scientific method, declared perfect by Immanuel Kant, may be drawn from the course of his achieved demonstrations and results, rather than from his specific statements. In the latter, however, the thought of generalization is pronounced, as befitted Newton's supreme achievement, the demonstration of that which until recently has been held the furthest and most securely established generalization in astronomy or physics, to wit, the universal fact (or law) of gravitation.

Says Newton, for example : " Natural Philosophy consists in discovering the frame and operations of Nature, and reducing them, as far as may be, to general Rules or Laws—establishing these rules by observation and experiments, and thence deducing the causes and effects of things." [1]

---

[1] This is the opening sentence of an undated " Scheme for establishing the Royal Society," by provision for the maintenance of its members " skilled in any one of the following branches of Philosophy." One notes the word *philosophy* where to-day we should say *science*. He gives the following classification :

" The Branches are—

" 1. Arithmetic, Algebra, Geometry, and Mechanics. . . .

" 2. Philosophy relating to the heavens, the atmosphere, and the surface of the earth, viz. Optics, Astronomy, Geo-

Newton is the classical example of a "natural philosopher" or mathematical physicist who would confine himself to the actual facts constituting the tangible scope of his inquiry, and to stating them under the most comprehensive generalizations or laws, which, however, shall be essentially descriptive rather than explanatory. Such a generalization rationalizes the facts, and broadens or carries backward their relationships.[1] Yet it makes no attempt

---

graphy, Navigation, and Meteorology ; and what relates to the magnitudes, distances, motions, and centrifugal forces of the heavenly bodies. . . .

"3. Philosophy relating to animals. . . .

"4. Philosophy relating to vegetables. . . .

"5. Mineralogy and Chemistry and the Knowledge of the nature of Earths . . . Rainwater, Springs . . . Gravity . . . Liquefactions, Volatility . . . Corrosiveness, Electricity, Magnetism and other qualities."

Taken from Brewster's *Life of Sir Isaac Newton*, vol. i. p. 102 *sqq.*

[1] A hundred years after Newton's death, William Whewell in his *History of the Inductive Sciences* writes, under the influence of this Newtonian conception : " Since the advance of science consists in collecting by induction true general laws from particular facts, and in combining such laws into one higher generalization, in which they still retain their truth ; we might form a chart, or table, of the progress of each science, by setting down the particular facts which have thus been combined, so as to form general truths, and by marking the further union of these general truths into others more comprehensive " (Introduction). Whewell's famous *History* is an important document of the scientific attitude of his time.

Laplace, in his *Système du monde* (first edition, 1796 : I am quoting from vol. i. p. 8 of the fifth edition, 1824), speaks thus in his clear intellectual French :

" Sur la terre, nous faisons varier les phénomènes par des

to state an ultimate or even an ulterior cause, lying behind the phenomena described in the generalized statement, for example, of the principle of gravitation.   As to those ulterior causes, " hypotheses non fingo," said Newton, " I do not make or invent hypotheses." [1]

Newton invented no hypothesis to account for gravitation.   Yet all his reasonings were based upon tacit assumptions or hypotheses, which taken together made up the Newtonian view of the universe, and of space and time especially.   Henri Poincaré says that every generalization is an hypothesis, and points out some of the hypotheses underlying Newton's law.   But assuredly all reasoning in physics, as well as in other sciences, proceeds from assumptions.

Passing on from the discoveries of Galileo and Keppler, Newton stated the law of gravitation and

expériences [experiments] : dans le ciel, nous déterminons avec soin tous ceux que nous offrent les mouvements célestes. En interrogeant ainsi la nature, et soumettant ses réponses à l'analyse, nous pouvons par une suite d'inductions bien ménagées, nous élever aux phénomènes généraux dont tous les faits particuliers dérivent.   C'est à découvrir ces grands phénomènes, et à les réduire au plus petit nombre possible, que doivent tendre nos efforts ; car les causes premières et la nature intime des êtres nous seront éternellement inconnues."

[1] Newton would not have posited any other hypothesis than God as an underlying explanation of all phenomena, an hypothesis for which Laplace is said to have seen no need. Newton composed a number of writings upon the Scriptures. See Brewster, *Life of Sir Isaac Newton*, vol. ii. pp. 324-359.

the laws of motion, which were to stand for centuries as final generalizations.   He analysed and presented the conception of Mass.   His laws made for the unification of our apprehension of physical pheno-mena.   They were great adjustments, easements of thought.   Physical law became a certain relation between a present condition and the next, even a relation between the present state of the world or universe and that immediately to follow.

From this base physics masterfully advanced. Its fundamental principles were stated more explicitly and were firmly established by the labours of an international succession of great physicists.   By the middle of the nineteenth century these sweeping laws had become the funda-mental assurances of scientific thought—the law of gravitation ; the laws of rest and of uniform motion in a straight line ; the law of uniformly accelerated motion, of the equality of action and reaction, the law of the conservation of energy and the palpable stability of mass, and that of the degradation of energy.   These governed events upon our little planet, and held good throughout the universe. Supported and carried into application through brilliant physical and chemical experiments, they reigned as securely as the geometry of Euclid.

But the discoveries of the last forty years, with the hypotheses framed to co-ordinate or account for them, have shaken these fundamental principles, and have shown the inadequacy of our accepted

mechanics to account for recently revealed phenomena. Conceptions of mass and matter have
changed and our ideas of physical energy and action.
Perhaps the revolution began with the discovery of
X-rays, of the electron and of radioactivity. Revela-
tions followed of the composite character and action
of atoms. And the principle of relativity has been
devised as the universal interpreter and reconciler
of phenomena.

It may be that the fundamental laws of thermo-
dynamics—the conservation of energy, and Carnot's
principle of its degradation—will endure ; but the
stable maintenance of mass is no longer accepted
for bodies moving in high velocities ; and the
tendency is to identify mass with energy, and energy
with electricity. At all events, the Aristotelian
conception of matter as material substance no
longer obtains in physics. And the Galilean-
Newtonian laws of motion seem now restricted in
their application to bodies moving at comparatively
low velocities, and, even as applied to such, may fail
in absolute accuracy. Finally, gravitation is under
revision.

Needless to say, the geometry of Euclid no longer
reigns alone. Other systems, based on opposing
postulates, or on a profounder mathematical analysis,
have won equal recognition.

The revolution is from the bottom upwards.
For the science of mechanics is fundamental to other
physical sciences ; and physics is equally funda-

mental, as in its treatment of the nucleus and electrons of the atom.

The feeling or idea of extension in space and of the flow of time is intimately part of our perceptive natures ; it belongs to our inheritance of conjoint bodily and psychic habits and necessities. But science has dispelled the idea of absolute space in which we perceive extension. Space has lost its absoluteness, one might say, its stable and independent existence. Time has suffered a like change, and has been harnessed to space as a fourth dimension of all phenomena. We are driven far to sea from Newton's anchorage :

" Absolute, true, and mathematical time, taken in itself and without relation to any material object, flows uniformly of its own nature. . . . Absolute space, on the other hand, independent by its own nature of all relation to external objects, remains always changeless and immoveable."

So spoke Newton, but now we listen to Henri Poincaré, the great apostle of relativity : " Space is amorphous, and the things that are therein alone give it form." " Whoever speaks of absolute space uses a meaningless phrase." " Space is only a word, which we have believed a thing." [1]

[1] *The Foundations of Science* (New York, 1913)—a translation of Poincaré's *Science and Hypothesis, The Value of Science,* and *Science and Method,* which Poincaré published between 1903 and 1912, the year of his death. The above citations are from Poincaré's preface (1912) and from pp. 413 and 417.

In these discussions one's thought often will revert to

Mass also has become unstable : " It is necessary to admit that bodies in motion undergo a uniform contraction in the direction of the motion." [1] " Matter seems on the point of losing its mass, its solidest attribute, and resolving itself into electrons. Mechanics must then give place to a broader conception which will explain it [matter], but which it will not explain." [2] Recent results would give rise to " an entirely new mechanics, which would be, above all, characterized by this fact, that no velocity could surpass that of light." [3]

Before the name of Einstein was heard, his great forerunners in mathematical physics had built up the supports across which he was to throw the vault unifying the structure.   I will not attempt to follow the train of experimental discovery and consequent modification of scientific conviction and speculation, which have led on to Einstein and in great part

---

Kant's conceptions of the subjectivity of time and space. One will bear in mind, however, that for Kant time and space were categories of the understanding—of the human apprehension of the outer world. In the new relativity they are components or elements of the actual facts perceived.

[1] *The Foundations of Science*, p. 307.

[2] *Ibid*. Poincaré's preface.

" Absolute space, absolute time, geometry itself, are not conditions which impose themselves on mechanics ; all these things are no more antecedent to mechanics than the French language is logically antecedent to the verities that are expressed in French."   *Ibid.* p. 93 (1902).

[3] *Ibid*. p. 312. For the inertia of bodies (opposed to the causes accelerating their motion) becomes infinite as the motion approaches the velocity of light.

forestalled the principles ascribed to him.[1] It is for us laymen to be on our guard against finding in him a too miraculous originality, while we accept the judgement of physicists and mathematicians as to his genius.

What is called " the classic principle of relativity " goes back to Newton, to wit : No mechanical experiment made on the earth can demonstrate the absolute and uniform velocity of this globe. Only its movement in relation to a star assumed to be fixed, the sun for example, can be determined. This statement may be generalized as follows : The laws of mechanics are not affected by the absolute velocity of the system in which they hold good, so long as this velocity remains constant.

Wrote Poincaré in 1901 : " By means of optical and electromagnetic experiments within a system in motion, it is impossible to discover the movement of translation of the system with reference to the ether." He also wrote, apparently in 1902 : " The state of bodies and their mutual distances at any instant, as well as the velocities with which these distances vary at this same instant, will depend only on the state of those bodies and their mutual distances at the initial instant and the velocities with which these distances vary at this initial instant ; but they will not depend either upon the absolute initial position of the system, or upon its

[1] Clearly given in Lucien Fabre's *Les Théories d'Einstein*, chap. ii. (Paris, 1922).

absolute orientation, or upon the velocities with which this absolute position and orientation varied at the initial instant." [1] He calls this the law of relativity—*la loi de relativité*. He wrote, perhaps ten years later :

" It is impossible to escape the impression that the principle of relativity is a general law of nature, that one will never be able by any imaginable means to show any but relative values, and I mean by that not only the velocities of bodies with reference to the ether, but the velocities of bodies with regard to one another." [2]

It is not easy for those of us who are neither mathematicians nor physicists to grasp the import of these last statements of Poincaré. Still more difficult will it be for us to grasp any idea of Einstein, who is altogether a mathematician. We are forced to gain such notion as we can of him from popular expositions.[3] His proofs are beyond our comprehension ; I confine myself to such of his shattering and then reconstructive propositions as may carry for myself and my readers some glimpse of fugitive meaning.

The work of Einstein, in so far as his conclusions seem likely to be held valid, has shown the need of

---

[1] *Foundations, etc.*, p. 85.

[2] *Ibid.* p. 501.

[3] Personally I have found most luminous *Einstein et l'univers*, by Charles Nordmann, Astronomer in the Paris Observatory (Hachette, 1921). It is translated by J. M'Cabe (New York, H. Holt & Co., 1922).

a fundamental revision of the Newtonian conception of space and time and gravitation, with sundry of the accepted principles of dynamics. Possibly its more transcendent importance—again in so far as it may hold valid—lies in its reconstruction of the principles of our understanding of the world.

It is his purpose to state the laws of Nature in such form that they may hold true for all observers, though the observers form part of different systems or frames of reference, which may be moving in different directions and at different velocities. Says he : " If, relative to K, K' is a uniformly moving co-ordinate system devoid of rotation, then natural phenomena run their course with respect to K' according to exactly the same general laws as with respect to K." This, he says, is the " restricted " principle of relativity.

But as no bodies in the universe fulfil these conditions of uniform and non-rotary movement, he subsequently devised a more universal formula, called the general principle of relativity : " All frames of reference are equivalent for the description of natural phenomena, or for the formulation of the general laws of nature, whatever may be their state of motion " : or again, " The general laws of nature are expressed through equations, which hold for all systems of co-ordinates." [1]

[1] " Co-ordinates " are the magnitudes which determine the position of a point ; e.g. latitude and longitude are the co-ordinates or magnitudes which determine the position of a point on the earth's surface.

These statements, which we may vainly struggle to understand, seem to make the frame of Einstein's system. Perhaps more intelligibly his general principle of relativity has been stated thus : " All systems of reference are equivalent for expressing natural laws, and these laws are invariant to any system of reference to which they are related. That means in effect : there are relations between objects of the material world which are independent of the one who observes them, and especially of his velocity. Thus, when a triangle is drawn on paper, there is something in the triangle which characterizes it and which is identical, whether the observer passes very quickly or very slowly, or at any speed and in any direction whatsoever, beside the paper." [1]

With Einstein, matter, mass, and energy tend to become mathematical equivalents, and are subject to the same physical laws. Poincaré had already found it necessary to " admit that bodies in motion undergo a uniform contraction in the direction of the motion." [2] The last is one of the well-known Einstein tenets, and may be related to his general proposition that " the geometrical properties of space are not independent, but are determined by matter." This signifies, for instance, that the ratio $3 \cdot 14159 +$ of the radius of a circle to its diameter varies with the gravitational field, and

[1] Nordmann, *o.c.* p. 207 (Eng. trans., p. 228).
[2] *Foundations, etc.*, p. 307.

would alter, let us say, in the neighbourhood of the sun.

With all the advocates of relativity, whether they follow Einstein or in part diverge from him, time and space have ceased to be absolute and distinct entities. They have united with their contents of mass or electromagnetic energy; and in thus becoming part of their contents, they have become part and parcel of each other. Time has become that necessary additional dimension or magnitude which is demanded by actuality, or, in other words, by the constantly energizing action which constitutes the universe. There can be no spacial actuality, manifestation, or event, without the component of time. Not merely does time enable the action to be or continue as a distinguishable duration; it enters and becomes a quality or dimension of whatever makes or constitutes this space-time action.

There can be no statement of laws valid for all the phenomena of the physical world unless there be an affinity or uniformity of quality and character among the phenomena. Physical science endeavours to refrain from speculating whether beneath this likeness of character among physical phenomena there is, or subsists, an underlying or all-pervading unity of Nature or the Universe. But science always has insisted, and the new theory of relativity insists with even broader and more significant intent, upon some sufficient likeness or uniformity in the phenomena investigated, which shall make possible the formulation of laws or descriptions of action which shall be universally applicable.

Thus the new relativity, with Einstein as its protagonist, has brought to likeness, or mutual conformity, mass, matter, and electromagnetic energy, until they have become interchangeable or equivalent manifestations of each other. Only through this principle of equivalence can it recognize the old law or laws of the conservation of mass, matter, and energy. Only through this has it been enabled to advance still further and assimilate weight and inertia and gravitation, and posit or describe their action under the same formula or law.

A linkage between space and time lies in velocity, which traverses space and requires time to do it in. Or, better, we may say, velocity traverses or passes through both space and time. In the new scheme of relativity, the velocity of an object is the expression of the time required to traverse a space, relatively to the observer, or of the time required for the observer to traverse a space relatively to the object, and with the seconds of his chronometer shortened according to the velocity of his motion. Since the object, or person, in motion is also held to shorten in proportion to the velocity, time and space diminish together as the velocity of the observer increases, and lengthen with the lessening of his speed.

Inertia is a universal feature of matter : when

matter is at rest, a force is needed to set it in motion, and when in motion, a force is required to stop, or accelerate, or deflect that motion. From Newton's time, the inertia of a body has been measured by its mass. According to the mechanics of Galileo and Newton, if a constant force be applied to a body, its velocity acquired at the end of one second will be doubled at the end of the second second, and so on. But the new physics has proved that there can be no velocity exceeding that of light, or 186,000 miles a second ; and that in consequence the velocity of a body acted on by a constant force does not continue to increase at the same rate, but at a rate which is constantly diminishing. For the mathematical argument has proved that as the speed increases (noticeably, of course, in the high velocities) a greater resistance is offered to the accelerating force. This means that the mass or the resistant energy of a body is not stable, but increases with its velocity, approaching infinity as the velocity of light is approached. Accordingly, the velocity of a body can never pass the velocity of light because its infinitely increased mass would then offer an infinite resistance.

It has also been shown that inertia is a property not only of palpably massive bodies, but also of electricity. An electric current, when it has over-come the initial resistance,[1] tends to continue, like

[1] More technically stated : " when the electric displace-ment is established against the impedance " (Mark Barr).

a body in motion, and when checked, may leap the obstacle. Accordingly, the particles of so-called " matter," which are charged with electricity, like electrons or cathode rays, would seem to have a dual inertia or mass. But further experiment upon the velocity of such particles shows them to act as though their mass were entirely of electromagnetic origin. That is found to vary with the velocity, and in correspondence (as we laymen are told) with the laws of the Einstein dynamics. Even a layman feels how hard a blow at classical mechanics and our accustomed thoughts of mass and matter has been struck by these new principles, called of relativity. One must be prepared to find that the inertia of the atoms, or rather of their component nucleus and electrons, is electromagnetic altogether. If so, *matter* has disappeared : and the electromagnetic mass and energy have become interchangeable.

Thus fundamental physical phenomena so far as recognized, not by our senses but by mathematical physics, are shown to conform to the same laws, or formulae or mathematical equations. Yet we still are moving within the purview and deductions of the " restricted " theory of relativity. Only when gravitation has been brought into the same fold will the unrestricted or universalized principle of relativity be reached.

We turn back to Newton's principle or law of inertia — that a body which is not acted on by any force maintains its velocity and direction unchanged.[1] This principle was grounded on mechanical experiment and astronomical observation. The planets seemed to maintain their direction and velocity in so far as they were not acted on by the attraction of other heavenly bodies. But since, in fact, none of them travelled in a straight line, but all of them in curves, Newton concluded that they did not move freely, but were subject to a central force, which he called gravitation. Hence these celestial bodies, as well as heavy objects on the earth, did not conform to the laws governing freely moving bodies, since they were subject to the distinct and *sui generis* force of gravitation, with its formula that bodies attract each other in direct proportion to their masses and in inverse proportion to the square of their distances.[2]

But gravitation or weight resembles inertia in being a quality of all bodies, and because the same number that tells the inertia of a body also tells its weight, in a given juxtaposition with an attracting mass. This number represents its mass. Newton appears to have made no further use of the striking fact that the inert mass and the weight of bodies are expressed by the same number. But Einstein saw in it the chance to join the law of gravity with the other physical laws.

Objects of all kinds, light and heavy, fall with

[1] I am now following the exposition of chaps. v. and vi. of Nordmann's *Einstein et l'univers*, already mentioned.

[2] Clearly Newton's law takes no account of the changes in the mass of bodies due to their motion.

the same speed, at least in a vacuum ; and not with a speed corresponding with their masses. Einstein concluded from this that weight or gravity was not a force, but a property of space in which bodies move freely.

A man, falling in space, falls with an accelerated motion, like any other object. He will not feel the weight or pressure of his own body, nor the pull of gold and silver coins in his well-filled pocket. For the coins, like the man's own body, have lost their weight, and no longer exert a pull. For himself and all his accoutrements, the accelerated falling motion has taken the place of the weight which he experienced while standing on the earth, holding his coins in his hand.

This is an instance of Einstein's " principle of equivalence," by which a properly accelerated motion does away with the noticeable effects of gravity : the two become indistinguishable. A person standing in a cage resting at an immense distance from earth and sun and stars would feel no weight or gravitation. But if his cage were drawn aloft at a speed constantly accelerated at the rate of the constant acceleration of a falling object near the earth, he would have the same sense of weight that he had on earth.

The conclusion is that the weight or gravitation of a body cannot be distinguished from its inertia. The mass which causes inertia and the mass which causes weight are one and the same.

Light itself is proved to be no exception to these laws or qualities of space—of space far distant from massive bodies and of space within their gravitational fields. It is only in remote inter-stellar spaces that light may be thought to travel in " a straight line " as we understand the phrase. In those parts of the universe where there is gravitation its path is curved like that of massive objects. Within the gravitational field of any massive body, light falls toward that body at the same rate per second as any solid projectile. A projectile, as we know, near the surface of the earth describes a parabolic curve, which is palpable enough and easily measured because of the comparative slowness of the projectile. The projectile, for example, may be taken to advance a hundred feet while it falls one foot toward the earth's surface. If it were going at a far higher rate of speed it might travel so many feet per second that its accelerated fall per second, according to the earth's gravitation, would not land it on the surface of the earth at all ; but it would continue its slightly curved path far into space.

The path of light travelling at the highest speed known to science is but very slightly curved by weight or gravity when within the gravitational field of any massive body, although it will fall toward that body the same distance per second as some slow moving missive. It is but recently that the curve of light—the light of a star passing close by the sun in a solar eclipse—has been calculated from astronomical observations.

Hitherto, and for most purposes still, a ray of light in a homogeneous medium has been taken as our standard of a straight line. Such a straight line is, or was, the shortest distance between two points, and two such lines, in the same plane, might be parallel and never meet. But now, under the reasonings of a new geometry, and the acknowledged curvature of our standard of straightness, a contrasted aspect of the problem is presented. For two concurrent rays, parallel for the nonce as they start from their sources, will be differently affected in their passage by their relative proximity to some star which they pass at different distances. Hence they will cease to be parallel, and finally may meet.

A general conclusion, as before suggested, is that gravitation is not a force.[1] Rather in the neighbourhood of huge concentrations of matter the universe is as if curved, and freely moving bodies follow, as it were, curved lines, which are their shortest paths. Thus the planets, because near the sun, follow curved orbits in a universe that *there* is as if curved. These are their shortest paths; and though these orbits do not form a straight line, they make, as it were, a planetary or celestial *geodetic*, which is a curve

---

[1] There is another objection to regarding gravitation as a force, in that such a force operative between stars calls for an instantaneous effect, which means an infinite velocity. But there is no velocity greater than that of light.

near huge masses of matter, but might be almost straight in spaces remote from sun and stars.

Possibly these curves are comparable with the arc of a great circle on the surface of any globe, our earth, for instance, which ships follow when seeking the shortest route over the ocean. A ship sailing from New York for a port due east of it in Europe would not make the shortest possible voyage by steering due east, but by following a great circle and at first steering somewhat north-easterly. The great circle is the ship's geodetic. Regarding these high matters, those of us who are not mathematicians may be permitted to hold an open mind.

One word more, here at the end of our faltering remarks on relativity and Einstein. If we turn back to his statements of restricted and general relativity which seem to frame his theory, and thence retrace with him the way perilous, it may appear that his high course has really been a quest of some invariant, some absolute and unchanging factor in any observation or experiment, or in the universe considered as one system, that shall remain unchanged and the same for any observer whatsoever, placed in any frame of reference.

" Einstein's general position is that the group of interrelated phenomena which constitute the universe must have something of an invariant nature about them." Ordinarily—" The principle of the conservation of energy is perhaps the invariant most commonly used. If we have any system of moving bodies, which is self-contained, then, however the configuration of the system may be changing in accordance with dynamical laws, there is always a function, of the positions and motions at any time, which is not changing but preserving its value, and we call it the *total Energy*. It expresses an *intrinsic* property of the system, with a meaning which is in no way dependent on the particular manner in which we choose to measure the positions of the bodies at any instant." [1]

For a different and simple instance of an invariant, imagine that a passenger in a rapidly moving train drops a bottle from a window. As he looks at it from the moving window it falls, to his eye, perpendicularly on the earth. An observer, however, standing by the track sees it falling obliquely, carried forward by the motion of the train, and describing a parabola.

But there is one factor or magnitude in the action of the falling bottle which is the same for both observers; and that is the time-element, to wit, the time of the bottle's fall from a height of about six feet to the surface of the earth, under the effect of its weight, or the principle of gravitation. This time is the same for both observers, and would be the same whether the train were standing still or in the swiftest motion. For every unsupported object, within the field of the earth's gravitation,

[1] J. W. Nicholson, in *Problems of Modern Science*, ed. by H. Dendy (London, 1922), p. 23.

falls toward the earth the same number of feet per second, whatever be its velocity in relation to the surface of the earth.

This is a simple, almost infantile, instance of an invariant. The Relativists, as has been said, would go further, and seek some invariant or absolutely real factor, that shall not change its dimensions, and assuredly not its nature, with the changes in the observer's station. Perhaps Einstein has found this reality in the so-called *Interval* between events —microscopically reduced events—in the phenomenal world. It consists in a union of space and time in the four-dimensional world of nature, and is a difficult conception which I will not try to elucidate. Perhaps we may find a more readily tangible reality —something which shall not change with any change of observers—in the necessary fourfold ordering of events into right and left, backwards and forwards, up and down, sooner and later, the last being the completing time-dimension. This fourfold ordering seems really to exist in a world of four-dimensional phenomena.[1]   And the fact of it may be regarded as an invariant.

III

Pressure of Ultimate Problems

Newton's laws promoted the simplification of physical phenomena. They helped to order and

[1] See Eddington, *Space, Time, and Gravitation* (1921), p. 36.

unify them. They were great adjustments, easements of thought. They did away with impedi-
menta, and unburdened scientific thinking. It
would be hard to overstate the services they have
rendered to " natural philosophy." Yet even such
constructive enablements, while promoting profit-
able methods of studying nature and helping to
simplify scientific thinking, and thus contributing to the advance of physics, led to the uncover-
ing of intractable facts and more complicated
problems.

Newton disclaimed hypotheses—and used them.
So must all scientific investigators and constructors
of generalizations or physical " laws." Nowadays,
with broader experience, we seem likely to accept,
from new points of view, the ancient principle that
man the observer is, and cannot help being, the
measure of all things. Yet with important modifications of the old meaning. We should say of
course, though as a possible truism, that the human
mind must be the measure and standard of human
knowledge, and so of human perception and cognition of nature. It would now seem—but let us not
be too sure of it — that the new principles of
scientific relativity have carried the idea of relation, even of necessary relativity, into the phenomena themselves. At all events there seems to
be recognized an inherent relativity in the actual
conditions under which physical phenomena are
presented to our sense - impressions, and through

them to our more ordered perception and ultimate cognition.[1]

Is it to be henceforth true that in the universe nothing is independent and unrelated, absolute in itself ? but that everything (and not merely our perception of it) is conditioned on its relations to other phenomena ? For example, as Einstein would hold, and many others, that " the geometrical properties of space are not independent, but determined by matter " ? Then, why not by " energy " ? one queries.

Opinions differ as to whether this all-conditioning relativity enters into the phenomena themselves. If the Dutch mathematician, Lorentz, one of Einstein's rivals, held that moving objects are actually contracted in proportion to their velocity through the stationary ether, Einstein would seem to hold that though they are contracted in proportion to their velocities relatively to any observer, this contraction is only an appearance due to the laws of the passage of light. There are also those who hold that there is no such contraction of moving bodies, either real or apparent.

---

[1] Analogously, may there not always have been an inherent, an efficient and *saving*, relativity in the objects apprehended or conceived in philosophical opinion and religious conviction, rationalizing those objects in relation to the scope of thought and the conditions of human living then prevailing ? Prevalent conditions of thought and life constituted the " frame of reference " or " system " in respect to which those objects were apprehended and in which the resulting opinions or convictions were true.

It would seem then that any general assumption as to the inherent and actual relativity of all phenomena is still contested, or accepted in a variety of senses. It would also seem possible that in this discussion we are not very far from a consideration of the powers of the human mind to know the outer and so-called physical or material world—not far from a discussion of the ultimate problems of knowledge, not far from what is dubbed " metaphysics."

Putting aside for the moment this disturbing suggestion, it is clear to us all that the recent progress of physics and the advent of " relativity " have increased the effort required of the thoughtful physicist even to approach his subject. Relativity's pregnant suggestions are formidable indeed. Heretofore there was suavity in the consideration of nature, based upon a stable concept of solid underlying matter and the laws under which it manœuvred but did not change. That suavity has left us with the breach of those solid concepts. An immense effort of reconstruction is demanded. The more insistent-minded among the mathematical physicists are impelled to consider the ultimate data of that obvious and natural universe which supplies subjects for their calculations, investigations, and theories.

With what austerity this task may be undertaken appears in the work of the eminent English mathematician, A. N. Whitehead.[1] He addresses

[1] *The Principles of Natural Knowledge, The Concept of Nature, The Principle of Relativity,* Cambridge University Press, 1919, 1921, and 1922.

himself to those most general and fundamental concepts which determine the character of physics as a science. The discussion may be philosophic, but his " philosophy " " is solely engaged in determining the most general conceptions which apply to things observed by the senses. Accordingly it is not even metaphysics : it should be called pan-physics. Its task is to formulate those principles of science which are employed in every branch of natural science. . . . The philosophy of science is the endeavour to formulate the most general characters of things observed. . . . They must be observed characters of things observed. Nature is what is observed, and the ether is an observed character of things observed. Thus the philosophy of science only differs from any of the special sciences by the fact that it is natural science at the stage before it is convenient to split it up into its various branches. This philosophy exists because there is something to be said before we commence the process of differentiation. It is true that in human thought the particular precedes the general. Accordingly the philosophy will not advance until the branches of science have made independent progress. Philosophy then appears as a criticism and a corrective, and—what is now to the purpose —as an additional source of evidence in times of fundamental reorganisation."

" This assignment of the rôle of philosophy is borne out by history. It is not true that science has advanced in disregard of any general discussion of the character of the universe." [1]

Prof. Whitehead's discussion is to be devoted to the elucidation of nature as it presents itself to our sense-awareness, and becomes ordered in our perception and idealized or generalized in our thought. He is most resolutely set upon avoiding metaphysics.

" Nature is that which we observe in perception through the senses. In this sense-perception we are aware of something which is not thought and which is self-contained for thought. This property of being self-contained for thought lies at the basis of natural science. It means that nature can be thought of as a closed system whose mutual relations do not require the expression of the fact that they are thought about." [2]

In the Preface to *The Principles of Natural*

[1] *Relativity*, pp. 4 and 5. In *Concept of Nature*, p. 2, Prof. Whitehead says, looking at the subject perhaps from a more special angle : " A science has already a certain unity which is the very reason why that body of knowledge has been instinctively [?] recognized as forming a science. The philosophy of a science is the endeavour to express explicitly those unifying characteristics which pervade that complex of thoughts and make it a science. The philosophy of the sciences—conceived as one subject—is the endeavour to exhibit all sciences as one science, or in case of defeat, the disproof of such a possibility."

For the philosophy of science, it seems almost a pity not to take up again the old term " Natural Philosophy," which in Newton's time meant science in general. Prof. Whitehead uses this old term frequently.

[2] *Ibid.* p. 3 ; see *ibid.* pp. 30, 46.

Knowledge he says : " We are concerned only with Nature, that is, with the object of perceptual knowledge, and not with the synthesis of the knower with the known. This distinction is exactly that which separates natural philosophy from metaphysics. Accordingly none of our perplexities as to Nature will be solved by having recourse to the consideration that there is a mind knowing it. Our theme is the coherence of the known, and the perplexity which we are unravelling is as to what it is that is known."

Again : " It is the philosophy of the thing perceived, and it should not be confused with the metaphysics of reality of which the scope embraces both perceiver and perceived."

So Prof. Whitehead will have nothing to do with " reality " or with the power of the human mind to know nature. Quite consistently he recognizes no such things as " secondary qualities," which are only in perception : " It seems an unfortunate arrangement that we should perceive a lot of things that are not there." " For natural philosophy everything perceived is in nature. . . . For us the red glow of the sunset should be as much part of nature as are the molecules and electric waves by which men of science would explain the phenomenon." [1]

In a very interesting passage Prof. Whitehead recognizes that the actual phenomena reflected in

---

[1] *Concept*, etc., pp. 27, 29.

sense-awareness do not exhaust the significance of the natural world : " Nature is the system of factors apprehended in sense-awareness. But sense-awareness can only be defined negatively by enumerating what it is not. Divest consciousness of its ideality, such as its logical, emotional, aesthetic, and moral apprehensions, and what is left is sense-awareness. Thus sense-awareness is consciousness minus its apprehensions of ideality. It is not asserted that there is consciousness in fact divested of ideality, but that awareness of ideality and sense-awareness are two factors discernible in consciousness. . . . It is perfectly possible to hold, as I do hold, that nature is significant of ideality, without being at all certain that there may not be some awareness of nature without awareness of ideality as signified by nature. It would have, I think, to be a feeble awareness. Perhaps it is more likely that ideality and nature are dim together in dim consciousness. It is unnecessary for us to endeavour to solve these doubts. My essential premise is that we are conscious of a certain definite assemblage of factors within fact and that this assemblage is what I call nature. Also I agree entirely that the factors of nature are also significant of factors which are not included in nature. But I propose to ignore this admitted preternatural significance of nature, and analyse the general character of the relatedness of natural entities between themselves." [1]

[1] *Relativity*, pp. 20, 21.

Blank misgivings of a creature
Moving about in worlds not realized !

—such would be the state of physical science limited
to sense-awareness and the direct perception of the
natural world. Be that as it may, and whatever
are the thoughts of Prof. Whitehead touching
subjects avoided by his argument, there seem to
be two flanks to his attack upon what he calls " the
bifurcation of nature." He discards the Aristotelian
conception of matter and attributes, although showing the historical reasons for it, and noting that it
corresponded only too well with a rational and
natural way of looking at things and indeed grew
out of it. This conception of substance and attribute
is one horn of the bifurcation. The other is its
psychological correlate, to wit, the whole inter-
minable argument as to the powers of the mind to
apprehend the external world. " There is now
reigning in philosophy and in science an apathetic
acquiescence in the conclusion that no coherent
account can be given of nature as it is disclosed
to us in sense-awareness, without dragging in its
relations to mind. The modern account of nature
is not, as it should be, merely an account of what
the mind knows of nature ; but it is also confused
with an account of what nature does to the mind.
The result has been disastrous both to science and
philosophy, but chiefly to philosophy. It has
transformed the grand question of the relations
between nature and mind into the petty form of

the interaction between the human body and mind." [1]

So, then, the phenomena of nature are to be taken simply as they present themselves to sense-awareness and in perception, and finally as they are when cogitated in the mind as to their relationships and causes. It may be remarked that while Prof. Whitehead refuses to discuss the power of the mind to know nature, he has much to say regarding its action upon the phenomena presented to sense-awareness. In other words, a good part of his work is devoted to the discussion of the action of the mind in converting the crude evidence of the senses into orderly scientific apprehension or knowledge. One might say that his argument continually backs around from a discussion of natural phenomena as data of sense-awareness to a consideration of the classifying and inter-connecting method and action of the mind in apprehending them. If so, are we not very close to a discussion of the power of the mind to know nature ?

Whatever temerity leads me to say of Prof. Whitehead is said with realization of the likelihood that I may misunderstand his interesting, but difficult, exposition of the fundamental concepts of natural philosophy. We proceed with him a little further. He feels that " the determination of the meaning of nature reduces itself principally to the discussion of the character of time and the

[1] *Concept,* etc., p. 27.

R

character of space." [1] Or, as he says elsewhere,
" The properties of time and space express the basis
of uniformity in nature which is essential for our
knowledge of nature as a coherent system. The
physical field expresses the unessential uniformities
regulating the contingency of appearance. In a
fuller consideration of experience they may exhibit
themselves as essential; but if we limit ourselves
to nature there is no essential reason for the particular nexus of appearance." [2]

" The homogeneity of time with space arises from
their common share in the more fundamental quality
of extension which is a quality belonging exclusively
to events. By extension I mean that quality in
virtue of which one event may be part of another,
or two events may have a common part. Nature
is a continuum of events so that any two events are
both parts of some larger event." [3]

The " spatio - temporal relationships " of one
event in nature to other events, constitutes their
passage or significance. In this process or passage
or significance of events, which is nature, there are
obvious differences between the spatial and temporal
elements; which will also hold good on ultimate
analysis. Among these is the temporal antecedence
and subsequence in the passage of events, which
exists independently of any time-system.

All nature is related and co-ordinated : " No-

---

[1] *Concept*, etc., p. 33.
[2] *Relativity*, p. 8.   [3] *Ibid*. p. 67.

thing in nature could be what it is except as an ingredient in nature as it is. The whole which is present for discrimination is posited in sense-awareness as necessary for the discriminated part.[1] An isolated event is not an event, because every event is a factor in a larger whole and is significant of that whole. There can be no time apart from space ; and no space apart from time ; and no space and time apart from the passage of the events of nature. The isolation of an entity in thought, when we think of it as a bare ' it,' has no counterpart in any corresponding isolation in nature. Such isolation is merely part of the procedure of intellectual knowledge." [2]

Further on the professor says, as with a sigh of relief—for one feels his longing to abandon ordinary language for mathematics : " This long discussion brings us to the final conclusion that the concrete facts of nature are events exhibiting a certain structure in their mutual relations and certain characters of their own. *The aim of science is to express the relations between their characters in terms of the mutual structural relations between the events thus characterized.* The mutual structural relations between events are both spatial and temporal. If you think of them as merely spatial you are omitting the temporal element, and if you

[1] How can anything be " posited in *sense-awareness* as *necessary* " ?

[2] *Concept*, p. 142 ; cf. *Ibid*. pp. 158-60.

think of them as merely temporal you are omitting the spatial element. Thus when you think of space alone, or of time alone, you are dealing in abstractions, namely, you are leaving out an essential element in the life of nature as known to you in the experience of your senses." [1]

Mathematical physics is the most austere of sciences. Its comparative lack of juiciness is owing to its strenuous endeavour for precision, and for the simplification, even the highly abstract simplification, which precision may demand. Says Prof. Whitehead : " The more ultimate sciences such as Chemistry or Physics cannot express their ultimate laws in terms of such vague objects as the sun, the earth, Cleopatra's Needle, or a human body. Such objects more properly belong to Astronomy, to Geology, to Engineering, to Archaeology, or to Biology. . . . Where does Cleopatra's Needle begin and where does it end ? Is the soot part of it ? Is

[1] *Concept*, p. 168. (The italics are mine.) The same passage proceeds to point out why it is not paradoxical to hold that what we mean by time or by space under one set of circumstances differs from what we mean by time or space under another set of circumstances ; for " space and time are merely ways of expressing certain truths about the relations of events . . . under different circumstances there are different sets of truths about the universe which are naturally presented to us as statements about space. . . . The modern theory of relativity has arisen because certain delicate observations, such as the motion of the earth through the ether, the perihelion of Mercury, and the positions of the stars in the neighbourhood of the sun, have been solved by reference to this purely relative significance of space and time."

it a different object when it sheds a molecule or when its surface enters into chemical combination with the acid of a London fog ? The definiteness and permanence of the Needle is nothing to the possible permanent definiteness of a molecule as conceived by science, and the permanent definiteness of a molecule in its turn yields to that of an electron. Thus science in its most ultimate formulation of law seeks objects with the most permanent definite simplicity of character and expresses its final laws in terms of them." [1]

And finally, with Prof. Whitehead, we note that ultimate simplicity never lies in the phenomena of nature as they appear to our senses ; but in the unapparent, and as it were causal elements, which science infers, or more happily has demonstrated, like the nucleus and electron of the atom or the component parts of the living cell. It is the bewildering and changing character of visible things that to-day, as in the days of Thales and Anaximander, drives the questing scientific spirit back through the changing apparent to the underlying cause.[2]

From failure to reach consistent conclusions upon nature through direct speculation, the Greeks were pushed to the sheer intellectual attempt to construct in thought a coherent scheme of things. Their search for that simplicity and order in the natural

---

[1] *Concept*, etc., p. 171 ; cf. *Principles*, etc., pp. 185-86.
[2] Cf. *Ibid.* chap. xvi.

world, which their minds insisted on, brought them to those ultimate reasonings which spring as much from the necessities of the mind as from its synthesis of experience.

The same impulses beat upon science to-day. Modern mathematical physics proceeds from an immense base of experience and systematic observation of the phenomena of our little rolling globe and the infinite moving stars. It, too, must endeavour to think the results of its observations and experiments, and so analyse and arrange them according to the still persisting logical needs and insistencies of thought. In so doing it converts its experience into intellectual harmonies. And occasionally, when doubting of the correspondence between such logical constructions and the actual phenomena of the terrestrial and celestial worlds, physics may be impelled to consider the power of the human faculties either to perceive and know the outer world or even to think it rationally.

Here science and philosophy are fellows, and one might add to them natural theology, or nature's demonstration of the divine, as another path leading to the same summit. For it would seem that with the profoundest and most passionate seekers — prophets, philosophers, scientists — the search cannot long proceed without the inward look and query touching the knowing mind and its power to know whatever it is searching out. According to the status and character of the quest and according to the sanguine or despondent temper of the seeker, he will seem to himself to apprehend clearly or obscurely or as through a phantasmagoria.

Man's love of the best is still the cause why the query as to his power to know cannot for long lay its insistency aside. Some natures will be satisfied with nothing short of the surest and profoundest truth they can attain. Science, directly investigating experimental science, is part of the whole story of the mind, and is affected by the temper of the age, related to the general state of knowledge and attitude toward fact, and concerns itself with various objects.

One is tempted to take a leaf from the new book of Relativity. The varying methods of endeavour after knowledge are part of the mind which seeks, and equally part of all the knowledge and opinion which it reaches. This is recognized to-day from new points of view. The method of the quest, the flowers by the way, the fugitive goal of reality so often grasped and lost, are of the new and actual relativity of knowledge in the knower. Plainly enough in the sciences having directly to do with human life—history, sociology, politics, psychology —the fund of knowledge or opinion is drenched with relativity. In the physical sciences — astronomy, physics, chemistry, biology in its many branches, even sacred mathematics—he is bold indeed who would deny that the whole mass of their attainment is conditioned in its truth by the faculties, methods, and temper of the scientific mind. And now a relativity of physical as well as mental fact, if the two be two and not one, an actual, factual, objective relativity is found throughout the universe of nature ; a relativity, note well, existent not merely in our apprehension of fact, but beyond that in the constitution of the universe. Our knowledge and the universe itself are alike somewhat Heraclitean.

Yet all this does not impair the impulse of physics toward reality, philosophic reality one might say. Although matter as metaphysical substance is discredited and physics insists upon investigating, not entities, but solely relationship and action, still it has made rather a noumenal world out of it all, which contrasts strangely with the world of our senses. It is still seeking reality and surest knowledge in relationships.[1]

Says Henri Poincaré : "We seek reality ; but what is reality ? The physiologists tell us that organisms are formed of cells ; the chemists add that cells themselves are formed of atoms. Does this mean that these atoms or these cells constitute reality, or rather the sole reality ? The way in which these cells are arranged and from which results the unity of the individual, is not it also a reality much more interesting than that of the

[1] " Pure logic and pure mathematics (which is the same thing) aims at being true, in Leibnizian phraseology, in all possible worlds, and not merely in this higgledy-piggledy joblot of a world in which chance has imprisoned us."—Bertrand Russell.

isolated elements, and should a naturalist who had never studied the elephant except by means of the microscope think himself sufficiently acquainted with the animal ? " [1]

" But what we call objective reality is, in the last analysis, what is common to many thinking beings, and could be common to all ; this common part, we shall see, can only be the harmony expressed by mathematical laws. It is this harmony then which is the sole objective reality, the only truth we can attain ; and when I add that the universal harmony of the world is the source of all beauty, it will be understood what price we should attach to the slow and difficult progress which little by little enables us to know it better." [2]

" Now what is science ? . . . it is before all a classification, a manner of bringing together facts which appearances separate, though they were bound together by some natural and hidden kinship. Science, in other words, is a system of relations . . . it is in the relations alone that objectivity must be sought; it would be vain to seek it in beings considered as isolated from one another." Science does not teach the true natures, but the true relations, of things.[3]

[1] Henri Poincaré, *The Foundations of Science*, p. 217, trans. by G. B. Halsted (1913).

[2] *Ibid.* p. 209.

[3] *Ibid.* pp. 349-50.   J. S. Haldane, *Organism and Environment* (Yale University Press, 1917), holds the view generally that chemical and mechanistic principles do not

Among the men of science who have pondered its aims and limitations, and have sought to construct a philosophy or rationale of the matter, was the late Ernst Mach. He thinks that " the business of physical science is the reconstruction of facts in thought, or the abstract quantitative expression of facts. The rules which we form for these reconstructions are the laws of nature. In the conviction that such rules are possible lies the law of causality. The law of causality simply asserts that the phenomena of nature are dependent on one another." [1]

Mach well may have had in mind Newton's refusal to form hypotheses touching the causes which may underlie the subjects of investigation. Again he says : " Physical science does not pretend

---

reach to the expression of the reality which is in the life of an organism—which, of course, every one admits for the present. He says, for example, p. 98 : " Looking at all these facts we are inevitably forced to the conclusion that the life of an organism, including its relations to internal and external environment, is something of prime reality, since it persists actively and as a whole, and moreover tends to do so in more and more detail with enlarging experience, so that life is a true development. What persists is neither a mere definitely bounded physical structure nor the activity of such a structure." On p. 109 he further suggests the inadequacy of mechanistic working hypotheses, while admitting their frequent necessity. It seems to me that perhaps they might almost be treated as metaphors, and be compared to the metaphors involved in the application of physical concepts to spiritual or mental states—e.g. the terms straight, oblique, upright, when applied to human conduct or character.

[1] Ernst Mach, *The Science of Mechanics*, p. 502 (trans. by McCormack, Chicago, 1907).

to be a complete view of the world. . . . The highest philosophy of the scientific investigator is precisely this toleration of an incomplete conception of the world and the preference for it rather than an apparently perfect but inadequate conception. . . . Physical science makes no investigation at all into things that are absolutely inaccessible to exact investigation, or as yet inaccessible to it." [1] Yet the investigator must check and standardize his results by occasional consideration of the world as a whole. He must not even limit his view to the considerations of his own science, exclusively viewed. "Purely mechanical phenomena do not exist; the production of mutual accelerations in masses is, to all appearances, a purely dynamical phenomenon. But with these dynamical results are always associated thermal, magnetic, electrical, and chemical phenomena. . . . [They] also can produce motions. Purely mechanical phenomena, accordingly, are abstractions . . . for facilitating our comprehension of things." [2]

He even disclaims the thought that scientific concepts correspond with reality: One should beware, he says, of ascribing "to the intellectual implements of physics, to the concepts, mass, force, atom, and so forth, whose sole office is to revive economically arranged experiences, a reality beyond and independent of thought . . . we should beware lest the intellectual machinery, employed in the

[1] *The Science of Mechanics*, p. 464.   [2] *Ibid.* p. 495.

representation of the world on the stage of thought, be regarded as the basis of the real world." [1]

Karl Pearson asserts more emphatically " that science is solely occupied with the invention of a conceptual model, and that often but a rough one. The new physics have attained no more than the old mechanics to any real explanation of the perceptual universe." [2]

Some scientists seem to hold a bolder creed : " Stated in its most sweeping form it [' the philosophy of physics '] holds that the universe is ultimately rationally intelligible [this sounds unconscionably like metaphysics !] no matter how far from a complete comprehension of it we may now be, or indeed may ever come to be. It believes in the absolute uniformity of nature. It views the world as a mechanism, every part and every movement of which fits in some definite, invariable way, into the other parts and the other movements ; and it sets itself the inspiring task of studying every phenomenon in the ultimate hope that the connections between it and other phenomena can ultimately be found. It will have naught of caprice in nature.

[1] *The Science of Mechanics*, p. 505. Mach speaks of the atomic theory as affording a mathematical model for facilitating the mental reproduction of facts.

[2] *Grammar of Science* (3rd ed., 1911), p. 355, note. Gravitation, relativity, and the electron at the other end of the scale, may be compared with the highest forms of art and literature, which also are conceptions, descriptions, modes of apprehension and expression. Is it all apprehension and description ? impression and expression ?

It looks askance on mysticism in all its forms . . . this philosophy is in no sense materialistic, because good, and mind, and soul, and moral values, which is only another word for God, these things are all here just as truly as are any physical objects, and with that kind of a creed they must simply be inside and not outside of this matchless mechanism."[1]

A mechanism which includes everything existing would naturally be " matchless," there being nothing left to compare it with. Our citation sounds a little like a " campaign document."

Scientists hold no general brief against philosophy. But they would not follow it in treating as self-evident propositions matters which experience should decide, nor in its refusal to put abstract ideas to the test of experiment.[2] Some of them are trying to construct a true, or at least workable, philosophy of nature. Like Prof. Whitehead, Wilhelm Ostwald has written sundry volumes on " Naturphilosophie," which he regards " as the generalization of the results of the natural sciences." Before him, Mach had called " the true endeavour of philosophy, that of guiding into one common stream the many rills of knowledge." [3]

There is, of course, the question whether the maker of such a philosophy of nature need or need

[1] R. A. Millikan, " Twentieth Century Physics," an address delivered Feb. 15, 1917.

[2] Mach, *Science of Mechanics*, p. 273, says that these errors infected Descartes' philosophy of physics.

[3] Preface to *Science of Mechanics*.

not consider the validity or character of his sensations and mental processes. It may be said that
such considerations involve the ultimate problems
of the understanding and the metaphysical discussion of the reality of the outer world. And this is
merely to baffle oneself with old unanswerable
questions. Such futility affords no comforting
sense of novelty and progress ! A philosophy of
science should avoid these problems and insist upon
itself as a sheer investigation and correlation of
the phenomena of the world as they are presented
to the senses of man and in his co-ordinating
thought.

But in thinking of these great matters how can
one help thinking one's very hardest ? or how can
one close the avenues of his thought to whatever
problem may intrude ? Here refusal and dis-
claimer may amount to recognition. How can the
scientific mind solve the puzzles of its sense-per-
ceptions, level the inconsistencies of its concepts,
and elicit from the tumult of phenomena the law
and order which is its faith, without in some way
considering the knowableness of nature ? This
perforce involves the cognate question of the power
or impotence of the human mind to know the
phenomenal world rationally, in its parts and as a
correlated whole.

The present reconsideration of physics and the
fervour of the new conceptions, seem to renew the
call for a philosophy of observation and experi-

mental inquiry. Such can no more leave unconsidered the character of the senses and the mind
than it can leave out the panorama of natural
phenomena. They are complementary phases of
the inquiry.

In an inquiry where no avenue of investigation
is closed and no test of knowledge left unrecog-
nized, why should not philosophy and science join ?
Neither can be ignored. Nor is there anything in
the courses of philosophy or science hitherto to
hold the two apart. Both have their valid progress
to show, as well as the part taken by each of them
in the furtherance of human knowledge and consideration. Because of the universality and pro-
fundity of its matter, philosophy may have reached
few conclusions. Yet it has constantly reviewed
its problems from broader vantage-grounds, and
in its search for truth has yielded to its votaries
that intellectual life which is its own reward. This
also is the best reward that science yields, while it
seeks by other methods a like goal of truth.

Incidentally the sciences show a larger accumula-
tion of knowledge and, some of them, a more even
advance. Yet which of them has not its scrap-
heap, or rather its shelf of bottles holding curious
abandoned doctrines which once were helpful ?
For in the sciences, as in philosophy, abandoned
doctrines have ushered in new truths and helped
to make them good. The Hipparchian-Ptolemaic
astronomy was well used by Copernicus, who

retained a part of its mathematical devices to account for the movements of the stars. Yet there was sheer contrast between the conception of the revolution of the sun and planets and fixed stars about the earth, and that of our planet making one with others in a dance around the sun.

Or to take a more finite illustration—in the eighteenth century, Priestley and Scheele, who held to the false phlogiston theory, rendered great services to chemistry. Their investigations of oxygen and other gases supplied materials for the further discoveries of Lavoisier, who discarded phlogiston very quickly.

Henri Poincaré compares the progress of science " to the continuous evolution of zoologic types which develop ceaselessly and end by becoming unrecognizable to the common sight, but where an expert eye finds always traces of the prior work of the centuries past. One must not think then that the old-fashioned theories have been sterile and vain."

IV

THE FIELDS OF SCIENCE

The divisions of natural science correspond with the habits or predilections of investigators and the more obvious distinctions between the different orders of phenomena in nature. Every one distinguishes between the things of earth and the celestial bodies above us. In our own world no one fails to note the difference between creatures that live and grow and the earth and water which support them. Then, manifestly, living things separate into plants rooted in the soil and animals moving freely in pursuit of food or pleasure. At the top of these is the race of men obviously enough.

The Greeks are the scientific ancestors of us all. From those earliest known times of scientific or philosophic stirrings in the Ionia of Thales and Anaximander, they held to the conviction of the oneness and law-abidingness of all nature. They were monists religiously, philosophically, and dynamically. This did not prevent their recognizing and following different branches of investigation, according to the natural grouping of the world's phenomena, until with Aristotle there is reached a practical classification of the sciences with their subjects. All the while they were convinced of the oneness of nature and the subjection of all its phenomena to natural laws. There was both unity and order in their world. And they could see one field of scientific investigation shade into another, as, for instance, when they noticed that the lowest kinds of animals are scarcely distinguishable from plants.

Our modern sciences had their mediaeval as well as Greek antecedents. But there was a resurgence of creative power in the first-hand investigations of the sixteenth century, which we are prone to take for the beginnings of modern science. The best of these sixteenth-century investigators, like Vesalius or Leonardo, had little thought of philosophy. Rather, they were hostile to it, from a contempt for the futile webs of scholasticism. But before and after them, there were others, Nicholas of Cusa for example, and, some generations later, Bruno, who were possessed by philosophy and at the same time absorbed in the world of science. Neither of them, however, was a great direct investigator like Leonardo or Vesalius.

With these two men and, in another direction, Copernicus the natural sciences of direct investigation seem to enter on a new life. Leonardo stirred the elements of them all; but the generations following him did not know the contents of his disordered manuscripts. In consequence, modern anatomy and physiology, for example, do not take their rise from his dissections of human bodies and the wonderful drawings of them, which are in the Royal Library at Windsor.[1] Vesalius must be held their founder. From his boyhood, in the Netherlands, his passion was the dissection of animals. And when he found his way to Paris he could not endure to hear the lecturer read from Galen, while rude assistants cut up the bodies of animals or men too clumsily to show whether the old text truly described the organs of the human body. Vesalius

[1] Now in course of publication by Vangensten and others (Christiania, 1911 *et seq.*).

would make his dissections for himself! He dissected before the lecturer, and, outside the lecture-room, went on dissecting animals and studying human bones in graveyards. At twenty-three he was made professor at Padua, where he conducted demonstrations directly from bodies under dissection. His *Humani Corporis Fabrica* was published in 1543, the year of the printing of the great book of Copernicus. It laid the foundations of modern anatomy and, less directly, of physiology, two kindred sciences which should depend upon dissection of human bodies and vivisection of living animals.

The latter, vivisection, means not merely penetrating observation, but acutely devised experiment, the skilful hand seconding the conceiving and inventive mind. Many times baffled in his search for a true understanding of the circulation of the blood, it was through years of vivisection that William Harvey finally worked out his demonstration of a matter so difficult that he had feared "it was only to be comprehended by God." *His* immortal *Exercitatio de Cordis Motu* was published in 1628.

"Harvey's work was a shining example for all future inquirers. The patient examination of anatomical features, if possible a comparison of those features in the same organ or part in more animals than one, the laying hold of some explanation of the purpose of those features suggested by the features themselves, and the devising of experiments, by vivisection or otherwise, which should test the validity of that explanation, that was Harvey's threefold method." [1]

By this method, the sciences of anatomy and physiology have since that time advanced. The nature and functions of bodily organs have been demonstrated with cumulative and reciprocally testing observations, conclusions, and experiments. Harvey's younger contemporary, the temperamental Borelli, brought the new physics of the Galilean epoch to play upon the problems of muscular power and movement. His friend Malpighi (1628–94) made use of the new-found resources of the microscope. By its aid he achieved an exhaustive study of the silkworm, discovered the capillaries in vertebrates, and investigated the minuter structure and tissue of the parts and organs of the body. [2] Then chemistry was called upon to aid the study of digestion and respiration. Variegated and manifold becomes the tale of physiology. Through decades and centuries the currents of investigation broaden and multiply. The great physiologists of the nineteenth century appear—Johannes Müller and Claude Bernard. Müller was an inspiration to hundreds of pupils; Bernard's scientific intelligence, his

[1] Sir Michael Foster, *Lectures on the History of Physiology* (1901), p. 53.
[2] Somewhat later the capillary circulation was more completely demonstrated by the Hollander Leeuwenhoek.

brilliant discoveries, his virtual reconstitution of the science, place him still higher.

Anatomy and physiology are typical of other sciences in their independence of philosophy ; and it is safe to conclude that modern science has never shown the affiliation with philosophy that was so characteristic of Greek science.

But modern science is Greek in its insistence upon order and natural law in the world of phenomena which it investigates. And its various branches in their progress since the sixteenth century, and never more markedly than to-day, tend toward a working confederacy and even an essential unity. As the sciences advance and extend their inquiries, they interlace with one another and render mutual aid. It is still more significant of their unity that, as each science pushes its research back to the causes or foundations of its subjects of inquiry, it tends to merge with other sciences.

To - day, for instance, only superficially, for convenience's sake, would a line be drawn between physics (including mechanics) and chemistry. And historically the line of great names—Boyle, Priestley, Lavoisier, Cavendish, Faraday, Dalton, to mention some of the most revered—which would appear in any history of chemistry, would also be included in a history of physics. These two sciences dealing with what still is masked under the name of inorganic nature, have become the bases of the biological sciences, which treat of the phenomena of living things. For example, "general physiology" is now based on physics and chemistry. One might even say that it largely is physics and chemistry. This is exemplified throughout the leading modern text-book on the subject, by W. M. Bayliss.[1] As the author says toward the end of his preface to the first edition : " My object then is to discuss the physical and chemical processes which intervene in these phenomena of [living things], so far as they are known. It must be kept in mind that all the methods available for the study of vital processes are physical or chemical, so that, even if there were a form of energy peculiar to living things, we could take no account of it, except when converted into known forms of chemical or physical energy in equivalent amount."

The plan outlined in these sentences is consistently carried through by Dr. Bayliss, and had already been illustrated brilliantly in the work of Claude Bernard.[2] A more general statement from

[1] *Principles of General Physiology*, 3rd edition, 1920.

[2] Claude Bernard (1813–78) states, in its ideal clarity, his conception of true physiological method : " La méthode expérimentale a pour but de trouver le déterminisme ou la cause prochaine des phénomènes de la nature. Le principe sur lequel repose cette méthode est la *certitude* qu'un déterminisme existe ; son procédé de recherche est le *doute* philosophique ; son critérium est *l'expérience*. . . . La méthode expérimentale n'est que l'expression de la marche naturelle de l'esprit humain allant à la recherche des vérités scientifiques qui sont hors de nous. Chaque homme se fait de prime abord des idées sur ce qu'il voit, et il est porté à interpréter les phénomènes de la nature par anticipation avant de les con-

an eminent biologist is as follows : " Biology—the science of all the innumerable phenomena .manifested by living things—has much in common with chemistry and physics. Indeed, in so far as living organisms carry on their functions and work out their destinies by chemical and physical means, biology may be looked upon as a sort of super-chemistry and super-physics, and obviously presupposes an adequate acquaintance with both these departments of learning. The living organism, taken as a whole, however, is something more than a mere physico-chemical machine. It possesses an individuality and exhibits a purposive behaviour which raise it to an altogether higher plane of existence, and in this fact, apart altogether from the question of convenience of treatment, lies the justification for separating biology from chemistry and physics and regarding it as one of the cardinal sciences." [1]

Another example of scientific amalgamation or inclusiveness is the science of geology, which sets no limit to the scope of its physical, chemical,

---

naître par expérience. Cette tendance est spontanée : une idée préconçue a toujours été et sera toujours le premier élan d'un esprit investigateur. La méthode expérimentale a pour objet de transformer cette conception *a priori*, fondée sur une intuition ou un sentiment vague des choses, en une interprétation *a posteriori*, établie sur l'étude expérimentale des phénomènes " (*Progrès dans les sciences physiologiques*, p. 78-79).

[1] Arthur Dendy, *Problems of Modern Science* (London, 1922), p. 113.

botanical, and zoological inquiries.[1]   James Hutton,
a Scotchman more famous since his death than in
his lifetime, did much to place the science on a basis
of comprehensive and searching observation and
induction from the actually observed data.   No
more than Newton would he have to do with hypotheses as to matters transcending observation and
calculation ; his geology was not concerned with
the origin of things.   His observations and his
argument could " find no vestige of a beginning,
no prospect of an end."   What he could see, or at
least fairly deduce from wide and careful study of
the rocks, was the operation through vast periods
of time of agencies of change still operative in the
world.   To quote his admiring friend and admir-

[1] A late American conception of Geology opens Pirsson
and Schubert's *Text-book of Geology* :
" Geology is that branch of Science which treats of the
Earth, comprehensively, as a subject of research and study.
It seeks to explain the origin of the Earth, especially in its
relations to other planets, and to the Solar System of which
it is a part ; it endeavours to account for its varied surface
features, for its atmosphere, the distribution of land and
water, its rivers, lakes, and seas, its mountains and plains.
It studies these features in the light of varied forces and
agencies operating upon them, and attempts to show their
history during long ages past.   It takes account of the
remains of plants and animals still existing in the rocks, it
aims to present a picture of the successions of living organisms
which have existed during past times down to the present."
One may remark that the study of our planet cannot be
confined to our planet, but must draw data from whatever
may be learned from study of other members of the solar
system.

able expositor, John Playfair : " In the planetary motions, where geometry has carried the eye so far, both into the future and the past, we discover no mark either of the commencement or termination of the present order. It is unreasonable to suppose that such marks should anywhere exist. The author of nature has not given laws to the universe, which, like the institutions of men, carry in themselves the elements of their own destruction. He has not permitted in His works any symptom of infancy or of old age, or any sign by which we may estimate either their future or their past duration. He may put an end, as He no doubt gave a beginning, to the present system, at some determinate period of time ; but we may rest assured that this great catastrophe will not be brought about by the laws now existing, and that it is not indicated by any-thing which we perceive." [1]

This passage is given by a great expander and vivifier of Hutton's work, Sir Charles Lyell, in his *Principles of Geology*, published in the years 1830, 1832, and 1833. It has for its sub-title, " An Inquiry how far the Former Changes of the Earth's Surface are referable to Causes now in Operation." It proved a great demolisher of the " Catastrophal Theory," eloquently expounded by Cuvier, which

---

[1] See Playfair's *Illustration of the Huttonian Theory* (1802). Hutton's *Theory of the Earth* was published in 1788. An English engineer, William Smith (1769–1839) perhaps first clearly saw the importance of fossils in determining the relative age of strata.

ascribed to violent catastrophes the changes in the earth and the extinction of past species of animals.

Lyell was the chief founder of so-called dynamical geology. The *Principles* opens with this definition : " Geology is the science which investigates the successive changes that have taken place in the organic and inorganic Kingdoms of nature; it inquires into the causes of these changes, and the influences which they have exerted in modifying the surface and external structure of our planet," and there follows a wonderful book which was to be revised and amplified through rapidly succeeding editions, but never to surpass the charm of the first draft.

" Another liability to error, very nearly allied to the [underestimation of the past time] arises from the frequent contact of geological monuments referring to very distant periods of time. We often behold, at one glance, the effects of causes which have acted at times incalculably remote, and yet there may be no striking circumstances to mark the occurrence of a great chasm in the chronological series of Nature's archives. In the vast interval of time which may really have elapsed between the results of operations thus compared, the physical condition of the earth may, by slow and insensible modifications, have become entirely altered ; one or more races of organic beings may have passed away, and yet have left behind, in the particular region under contemplation, no trace of their

existence. To a mind unconscious of these inter-
mediate events, the passage from one state of
things to another must appear so violent that
the idea of revolutions in the system inevitably
suggests itself." [1]

One reads this illuminating passage, and then
notes with interest that the author who did so much
to remove " catastrophes " from the agencies of
our geologic past, still kept his mind closed to the
intellectual need to eliminate them from the origin
of species as well as from their destruction. Dis-
cussing the subject of the variability and trans-
mutation of species in the *Principles of Geology*,
Lyell refuses to accept the arguments of Lamarck,
and comes to a final conclusion " that species have
a real existence in nature ; and that each was
endowed, at the time of its creation, with the
attributes and organization by which it is now
distinguished." [2]

Yet if Lamarck was rejected, no book did more
than Lyell's *Principles* to prepare for the reception
of Darwin's *Origin of Species* (1859) ; to whose views
Lyell signified his own adhesion in his last great
work, *The Antiquity of Man*, published in 1863.

Through the study of fossils geology links itself
to zoology and botany, the sciences of animals and
plants, and themselves to be included under biology,
the science of all living things. Recently it has

[1] *Principles of Geology*, vol. i. p. 118 (5th edition, 1837).
[2] The last sentence of chap. iv. of Book III. (fifth edition).

been felt that the division between botany and zoology tends to prevent the realization of the fundamental identity of physiological processes in plants and animals. But the division is still needed for descriptive classification.

Some portions of this chapter upon the working of the scientific mind will seem like fragments of a historical sketch, while other parts may appear as a layman's reconnaissance of recent scientific theories. My purpose has been merely to illustrate the age-long endeavour of the human mind to comprehend the world, an endeavour which has resulted in the amazing extension of inquiry and, we may say, of knowledge, forming and filling with quick thought the spacious avenues of science.

The increase of scientific knowledge and the unfolding of scientific inquiry proceed together, yet may not be the same. Increase of knowledge is most readily observed by following the course of a definite topic of investigation. An apt example would be the advance in the knowledge of electricity through the investigations of the last two centuries. In these pages, however, physiology has been taken as an illustration of the constant gain of knowledge in a definite field of research. As a concrete topic of study it has been surer in its advance, and less subject to reversal, than the far-reaching conceptions or theories of biological science. With respect indeed to any general theory, that of organic evolution for example, the vital question may be

whether it is fruitful, rather than whether it is true.

There is an overwhelming mass of converging evidence in favour of the evolution of the variegated world of organisms from more modest beginnings. This theory is generally accepted : the intellectual world is evolutionist. Some conception of evolution has become an attitude of mind not only with biologists, but with the students of the social, political, or historical sciences.

But there is less agreement among biologists to-day than there was fifty years ago as to the causes, means, or manner of this evolution. A happy result of this disagreement is the prodigious stimulation of inquiry to account for this evolution which is accepted as a general principle. For this reason one may say that the theory of organic evolution marks an epoch in the progress of scientific inquiry as distinguishable from concrete scientific knowledge. Knowledge is the suggesting and enabling element of inquiry, and inquiry is the means of increasing knowledge ; the two join in the goal of further attainment. But every inquirer feels the difference between his process of experiment and the known facts on which it proceeds, which differ likewise from the sought-for fact, the ascertainment of which shall crown his labour, and also serve to increase knowledge and point new inquiries.

The free and voluntary action of the human mind is the cause alike of the extension of its own

inquiries and the increase of its own living and reacting knowledge. With each expansion of knowledge the mind is enabled to extend the provinces of its free endeavour after knowledge infinite. Each discovery may lead it on ; and thus the action and attainment of the mind serve to point out its next advance into an ever enlarging sphere of intellectual freedom.

CHAPTER VII

ART AND LITERATURE

Man, the investigator, remains the measure and criterion of the truth of things which he discovers. His variegated knowledge of the world about him and the heavens above is the growing and amplifying base of the apex which is the knower. The final study of mankind still remains man.

The motives prompting physical inquiry tell more of the inquirer than do the results of his inquiry. His qualities are disclosed in his attitude toward fact and in the method and energy of his search. These human elements of science are intimately part of the seeker ; they represent his intellectual nature.

Touched with desire and volition, the intellect functions in philosophy and science. But beyond philosophy and science, there are other signal human activities which are more wholly engaged with human qualities and situations, and involve more palpably the interplay and action of sensitive and emotional as well as intellectual faculties. They spring from the impulse of men and women

271

to express their thoughts, their feelings, their passions. The rudiments of science lay in common habits of observation and practice; from these, through the larger curiosity of gifted individuals, advance is made to theory and ordered investigation. Likewise the beginnings of art[1] lay in the natural impulses and energies of expression, which also may bethink themselves and become purposeful, become descriptive, imitative, creative. The human mind transforms its expressive energies into vehicles of the thought and feeling which are consciously intent upon humanity, and are directing themselves to its consideration and to the endeavour to depict it in images and words. In this way the imaginative and creative arts arise, of poetry and music, sculpture and painting. Through them the whole spiritual nature of man, embracing intellect, imagination and feeling, works creatively, considering, judging, and, above all, interpreting and present-

---

[1] I must apologize for using the word " art "—it is more vague and heterogeneous in meaning than " philosophy." Though we improperly limit the term to sculpture and painting, we find that art has been many kinds of things, and has been actuated by a variety of motives springing from religion, from patriotism, from the love of beauty or the taste for comfort and luxury. I cannot pause for a disquisition on the meanings of the word *art*, or the *artes*; but will just remark that the use of the term in the sense of *Fine Art*, something essentially aesthetic, appealing to our sense of beauty or pleasure, appears to be the latest of its uses. Yet I fear it is in that sense mainly that I am about to use it. Though disapproving, we must to some extent in writing conform to the usage of our time!

ing human life in finished or ideal forms. The arts present man, either directly, or indirectly through rendering some phase of his physical environment in its effect upon human sentiment. They have been constant exponents of human life and progress, and universal factors of incalculable power.

All the achievements of humanity are in some sense expressions of the hero of the tale. Agriculture, industry, building, architecture, the crafts, social and political institutions, jurisprudence, philosophy and science, nay, religion too, reflect the nature of the creature that created them—a creature driven by need and instinct, yet still working with some measure of freedom. But far more intimately and wholly, imaginative literature and art mirror and present man. They are the most direct and explicit expression of his ideals ; they offer the most ample consideration of human life, of human faculty and its fateful limitations ; they estimate conduct and pronounce judgement ; they disclose the paths, show how men and women should press on, point out the pitfalls ; they unroll the folly which is sin and becomes fate ; they demonstrate and exemplify the sublimity of humanity ; they unfold and make luminous its beauty ; and they give joy to all men and women. They are the crown of life.

Their instruments are diverse : language for literature, form and colour for sculpture and painting, and for music, sound. Each art is cast by the properties of its medium. Yet their subjects

T

are drawn from human experience, and in substance are the same for all the arts.[1] Also in bringing their matter to expression, imaginative prose as well as poetry, and likewise painting and sculpture, follow the same fundamental method of embodying in the particular presentation that which is of general human significance. Thus the arts present the tale as well as summary of man. They are just as manifold and comprehensive as human life, and have kept step with the traditions and history of mankind.

The vocation of the arts is human self-expression ; and in the fulfilment of their task they furnish ample presentation of the qualities and conduct and progress of mankind. Conversely, they issue from the co-operation of intellect, imagination and feeling. Since their subject is the whole of man and every factor of his being and behaviour, these human expressional energies which are transformed to art must be of the whole man. Poetry and inventive prose, sculpture, painting, music, cannot be of the intellect alone. They cannot ply their task save through the co-operation of all parts and faculties of man—temperament, mood, feeling, emotion, as well as the form-giving intelligence. The whole man shares in these creations, his faculties working together, balancing, proportioning, and vitalizing one another in an harmonious autonomy which is of the whole man.

[1] Regarding music I speak uncertainly.

Nor should one suppose that, in the artist's work, the intellect gives orders to the imagination and feeling, while the imagination furnishes material, and feeling makes it live. Rather each is in and of the other in the work. There is no hegemony of one faculty, but an autonomy of the whole.

And as the arts have to do with the whole man, and issue from the whole man, they may be held to carry the broadest and surest truth. Truth for us men, human truth and validity, does not spring from the unchecked action of a single faculty ; but rather from the co-ordinated and mutually balancing action of them all. And so far as the arts are true literature and sculpture and painting and music, they interpret the facts and energies of human life in their truly adjusted values and efficient proportions ; they present life truly, illuminate its course and veritable outcome, implicitly teaching its lessons, or beguiling hearer, reader, beholder to its better understanding.

Art then is adequate for its expressional and interpretative function. Is it also free ? Do the human energies of self-expression act freely in producing poetry and imaginative prose, music, sculpture, and painting ? How far are works of art the free creation of the artist ?

One may answer that they represent the most complete autonomy of human action. The artist's mind draws imagination and feeling within the unity of its catholic functioning, and still works rationally. All the contributing faculties are imbued with the rationality of intelligence and share in the selective and constructive action of the whole. Through their balance, mutual control and adjustment, their union in co-operation, they move in a larger freedom than any one of them possesses by itself or could have attained alone.

Let us consider briefly wherein consists the freedom of the arts, beginning with architecture. This is not in itself a vehicle of human self-expression. Buildings speak articulately only through the painting and sculpture which adorn them and make clear such ideal purpose as they possess. The art of building springs from man's need of shelter. Our environment occasions this need and furnishes the means to meet it. The materials offered suggest the manner and form of construction. Climate and natural building materials call forth the common forms of building, which nevertheless are shaped by men using their wits. Useful buildings, like political institutions, are partly necessitated and partly the fruit of the freely devising mind.

An example is the modern steel skyscraper of our large American towns. The congestion of people and high cost of land furnish the need ; the earth provides the iron and the materials for tiles and bricks and plumbing. But what cunning human invention ! and what complex processes of scientific and mechanical discovery lie behind the power of using these materials thus ! There was congestion in the ancient city and the mediaeval town, squeezed inside the defensive city - wall. Here also was need for houses of several storeys, a need which was met by the craft and knowledge of the time working with stone and wood.

So much for buildings framed for utility. More noble and aspiring structures designed for a public or religious purpose reflect to some degree the pressure of environment, as well as the compulsions of human nature and the demands of society. The noblest of them are in every instance the culmination of a series of efforts to achieve a notable and beautiful form. The Parthenon or Santa Sophia or Chartres Cathedral are examples of this ; and in them the constructive genius of architect and decorator evinces itself most brilliantly. Mind and craft work in freedom, and press to their uttermost limits the possibilities of materials and media. One cannot ascribe to necessity the achieved form of any of these temples of the living God and the genius of man. Necessity did not shape the columns of the Parthenon, or give a subtle curve to its long line of architrave, any more than necessity designed the frieze or the figures of the pediments. No compulsion built the spires of Chartres or painted its windows.

But the people who will use these buildings, for whose pleasure and edification in a measure they are built, are possessed of a complexity of motives and religious convictions. These motives and con-

victions have had their history : long courses of
development are behind them, with occasional
torrential crises.   It is such collective convictions
that prescribe the purpose of Parthenon or cathedral ;
they will affect the form of each and supply the
subjects of its most speaking decoration.

Thus from the side of the people — priest and
laity—fine spiritual conceptions and a measure of
intellectually directed feeling influence the constructive and inventive genius of architect and
decorator, and so affect the structure of the building
and inspire its carved and painted decoration.   It
is not too much to say that all sorts of intellectual
and emotional energies have given form and meaning
to all great buildings and have lent them beauty.

In great sculpture and painting and in great
literature, usually the matter is given to the artist
or poet.   It has been made, as with the Greeks, by
the mythopoic fancy of the race, or, as in the
Christian Middle Ages, by religious thought and
feeling working over the contents of the Faith.
Artist or poet will give it visible or rhythmic form.

In the plastic arts, a sculptor or painter is
hindered or facilitated, according to his skill, by
the medium—stone or pigment—that he works in.
The men who carved the archaic statues of Zeus or
Athene were hampered by imperfect mastery of
their art.   Thus they were less free than Pheidias
who could do so much more with marble or gold or
ivory.   Neither did he invent his subjects.   The

mattei of Athene's birth or contest with Poseidon had been conceived : Pheidias, or some Pheidian sculptor, rendered it in creative freedom in the pediments of the Parthenon. With still freer facility he immortalized Athens' civic festival in a consummate frieze. Thus through his skill, the sculptor wins freedom for his genius. He can execute the free devisings, the plastic conceptions, of his mind.

Two thousand years later worked Michelangelo. He was the painter of his Faith's interpretation of the Old Testament Epic and of the Last Judgement. The matter came to him to be transformed in his creative, his dramatic, and dynamic soul ; and to be rendered by those mighty hands that knew no hesitation in the execution of his thought. His media of fresco or of marble were not impediments, but altogether fitting means and instruments. He worked in them as a free creative giant. That they did not hamper him appears from the fact that he was greater as painter and sculptor than as poet. Beautiful as his verses are, they are difficult to read, and betray the writer's effort to express his thought.

More originatively Michelangelo evolved the subjects of his sculptures on the Medici tombs. It was the plastic melancholy of his own thought that he eternalized in the sombre speculation of those recumbent figures. Here was free creation, however temperamentally impelled and darkened by old age and a hopeless political situation. Yet in all his works, the *furor* of his genius forced masses of thought and passion old and new into the matrix of his own nature, and from the transformed substance drew matter for his brush, his chisel, or his poet's pen. Raphael made his frescoed world out of a suaver and less drastic treatment of a like material. Every artist works with the data of his understanding and is impelled or moulded by the cast of his time. Yet though his mind be set in accepted knowledge, opinions, sentiments, he fashions his matter with a freedom commensurate with his genius.

We turn to imaginative literature, which for us, Europeans and Americans, is taken as beginning with the Greek and Hebrew mythologies. It will advance and expand through human and heroic legends, and the telling incidents of history : legends of deeds, legends of sorrow and mortality ; stories of ponderable fact like the founding of cities and the conquests of one people by another ; or disclosures of the experiences of the heart, as in Greek lyrics or the Hebrew Psalms. It will deepen its consideration of life in Greek tragedy, with Aeschylus, Sophocles, and Euripides, and in the odes of Pindar ; also in Hebrew Prophecy.

The Homeric Epics present human traits and life's stirring incidents in a kind of glancing beauty ; and the deeds of each hero are finished by a fitting fate. Tales of Troy had come to the great bards who sang them ; but their imagining minds created freely these consummate poems. From battle and action and revenge, comes at the end " peace of mind, all passion spent." After Achilles has granted Priam's prayer for the body of his son, and the old man and the hero have gazed in wonderment on one another, Priam sleeps on the couch in Achilles's tent, and the surgings of Achilles's grief for Patroclus are calmed. This great night scene is the epic fore-runner of the tragic purge of feeling, the tragic Katharsis which Aristotle sets out so thoughtfully in his *Poetics*. Homer knew it and rendered it in beauty—as with him all things make for beauty. So move the words and thoughts of Helen when she speaks of herself and Paris, " upon whom Zeus has set such evil fate that we shall be a theme of song— ἀοίδιμοι—to men in times to come."

'Αοίδιμοι ! As theme of song poetry accepts the sad and joyful content of life ; and touches it with beauty, through the words of Helen, or some passing incident. Odysseus at last has got the great bow in his hand, has strung it and twanged the cord, and " pleasantly it sang to his ear like the song of a little swallow." In this finishing touch the Homeric bard worked as freely as when he drew the lovely episode of Nausicaa.

Likewise the story of Atreus's accursed house came to Aeschylus—given him somehow. The *Agamemnon* universalizes it, presents it as the embodiment of the fate of evil-doers ; in the utterances of Cassandra it is made to reach the summit of tragedy. The mind of this titanic dramatist worked freely. He made his drama so, as he saw fit; he might have made it otherwise. Sophocles follows him, his genius freely choosing to round life out more completely in his *dramatis personae.* Euripides injects a bitterer gall of passion, and floods action with lamentation. Aristophanes shows life's laughter, often bubbling through an exquisite light beauty. And all the time sculpture was vying with verse in rendering the epic, the tragic, the more subtly emotional, and even the comic elements of life.

But why multiply proofs of the poet's freedom ? Any one of us can draw ample evidence from our own Shakespeare or Milton. In Shakespeare we can even tell what he invented, since sometimes we know the sources of his plays. There is no need to press a point which no one will gainsay. We may take it to be clear that the sculptor, painter, poet, or composer, works in freedom according to the measure of his transforming and creative genius.

Thus the arts mirror human freedom, human nature, and humanity's chequered progress. They are the humanities *par excellence.* The tale of them passes before us, a signal and exhaustless vision. In them Greece was and still lives. Expressionally and artistically Rome follows Greece, and then the Christian Middle Ages emerge, plying like arts of human expression. Achilles, Agamemnon, Clytemnestra, had been rendered in their life tragedies ;

now Roland and Siegfried fill the tale. And as the gods and heroes and civic events and personages once covered the temples, so the figures of Christ and Mary and the saints, as well as incidents of industry and harvest, place the full human story on the Cathedrals.

As the Middle Ages close, the poet Dante presents a final *summa* of their thought and feeling, rendering it through the concrete story of the experiences of his own life's journey, which for a full man may pass through hell and purgatory and paradise. Even while Dante is composing his *Commedia*, Giotto with less tragic depth, but with understanding and comprehensiveness, is painting humanity, its daily tasks, its virtues, its love and tears, into his religious frescoes.

The times advance, and change in temperament. In another country, Shakespeare, as no other man had done, dramatically renders the glory and vainglory of life, and the range of its alluring realities. He is English. The Frenchmen, Racine and Molière, will symbolize life dramatically as they and their auditors regard it. The great German, Goethe, too, will give life whole, though his renderings reflect the processes through which that absorbing ego fashioned the hopes and loves and tears, and the intellectual interests, of the men and women he passed among—or passed over—into the matter of his life.

These men, like Raphael and Michelangelo, were

among the Olympians of art—as Beethoven was. Around them and after them, throng myriads, writing, painting, composing works which reflect their makers and their makers' knowledge of humanity, and suit the tastes and temper of the day.

There is no end to the material. It waxes from age to age. Time's loom bids fair to be exhaustless. Art as well. It keeps pace, rendering every human mood, the grander and the lesser ways of life. Not buskined tragedies alone, nor the high triumphs; the minor, still universal, incidents of joy and pain, of love and hate, of holiness and sin press into poetry and story, and are carved and painted. Story turns to inventive fiction. Novels abound! In our modern time the arts have become catholic, democratic, inquisitive. They draw from all sorts and conditions of men. They inhale the intricacies of social situation, its embarrassments. They spy into the crannies. They estimate, portray, and interpret; they give us the scale of life, its fuller chords, sustained dominants and recessive burdens, its crotchets and quavers; the fugue of desire and joy, pain and aversion, the antiphony of life and death.

CHAPTER VIII

THE PROSPECT

Our brief and desultory review of the factors of human progress and the manner of their operation may well leave us wonderstruck at the progress and accomplishment of mankind. How short has been the time of this achievement ! All the sciences testify to the brief period during which man has been man upon the earth.

It is true, size and time seem to count for little ; things are more wonderful as they get smaller, like the nucleus of the germ-cell or the electrons of the atom ! Mind has no size at all, and changes instant by instant. Nevertheless, everywhere upon the earth, if not throughout the universe, successions of antecedents and consequents are to be traced, and of all such successions nothing is so wonderful as man.

He is but one out of myriad organisms. Men and women are animals in their origin and growth and propagation. Like other animals, and plants for that matter, they assimilate food and each individual grows through a process of cellular multiplication and plastic function : everywhere fundamentally the same process, and as astounding in the oyster or the germinating oak as in man. Yet in this general environment, and passing through like physical stages, man alone has become man. Having somehow reached his animal manhood, thereupon in the small space of historic or quasi-historic time, he has made the prodigious advance from savagery to his present state of complex civilization, as we call it.

Again, note well : the same physical conditions have surrounded, have nurtured, all animals and plants, and man has risen from all the rest.   Environment ! physical, economic conditions ! the laws of nature ! what have they made of snakes and bears and buffaloes, or even apes ?   Man alone seems to have defied or used them.

The evolution, or the descent, of *genus homo*, of *homo sapiens*, is taken not to have differed essentially in process and working factors from the manner of descent or evolution of other species.   But man alone became man : however descended, he alone has ascended.   One may think that somehow he must have been endowed with mind.

The fossil ants encased in amber indicate that some species have endured unchanged through geologic ages far exceeding the period of man and the higher mammals.   What then produced the rapid and comparatively recent evolution of the human body, or of the human mind and body ?

What could it have been (under God) but the plastic and planning mind of this creature constantly impelling it to new bodily activities, which in turn called forth some answering action of the mind ?

Perhaps no absolute separation is to be made between him and other animals; he may not be essentially different in kind. But infinitely in degree. His nervous structure is more complex, further developed; that is a fact, whatever be its bearing. But we may be sure that it is in his mind, and in the free action of his mind and the balanced autonomy of his whole nature, that man differs most from other animals. And whencesoever sprang the human mind, and howsoever it has developed till it has become the genius that it is in gifted individuals—howsoever this may have come to pass, the human mind, and not any physical environment or conditions, is the well-spring of human progress.

Hail to the human mind, and hail to man ! Hail to the progress of mankind ! And hallowed be our thought of the Power that made this divine creature. For creature is he still. Whatever we may think of man, we cannot think him as an initial self-creator. He did not start himself ! He seems the creature somehow of a god, a god who is spirit, who is love, who is all the valid qualities that can be found in man. Men may wallow, foolish and recalcitrant, in the pit from whence they have been digged; or the wiser individuals, perhaps responsive to the inner voice of the divine, may uplift their vision, which shall be ever larger and more free as further range is won. The disparate elements in the balanced autonomy of these finer natures seem to have joined their forces, ever making this advance the achievement of the whole man.

Whither does the tale seem to point ?

Only brisk and shallow minds profess to understand this great matter, profess to see what it all means, or deny all meaning to it. Most shallow and self-limited are those who discern physical law portending human chaos ; as if the vast evolving web of natural life, with its infinite adaptations and pervading beauty, should result in a meaningless confusion and a wrecking of that state of man which the long processes of nature—or the spirit of God—finally made possible. We simple folk do not fully understand it all, nor can we arrange everything in clear causal sequences, and declare the specific *rationale* of each event. We can only assemble such elements as we perceive of the stupendous movement, and ponder upon their values, while admitting in honesty that our judgements are likely to follow our temperaments.

We may profitably recognize that all sides and phases of the age-long human endeavour have a unity of origin in the action of the mind responding to impulses, all somehow homing in the individual. Yet we also recognize that the marvellous and many-sided human attainment has never been, and is not, the product or achievement of any one function or phase of human faculty or capacity or potency. It has not resulted altogether from the toil and effort of mankind to satisfy their material needs, so constantly expanding; it has not been altogether a sheer economic progress, nor dependent altogether upon the varying conditions of man's physical environment.

Nor has it altogether been the product of human reason working in its self-efficiency. It has not altogether sprung from the reason exercising itself in logic and metaphysics; nor from the reason, in conjunction with the perceptive faculties, prospecting the visible, tangible, ponderable, measurable worlds of inorganic and organic nature; investigating the bodily constitution of man and other animals, and delving into the minute and marvellous sources of his natural life. Nor has it altogether sprung from faculties of social adjustment, through which human groups have been formed and human societies, and states and governments, and economic, social, and political institutions. Nor has the progress of mankind exclusively and assuredly arisen from man's recognition of the moral law, or from his tremendous sense of physical and spiritual consequences, working through the fatal or benignant power of his acts, or through the retributive and rewarding efficiency of God. So far as we may see, it has not altogether resulted from religion, from the faith and spiritual impulses and certitudes of men addressed either to impulsive, arbitrary gods, or to God conceived and felt as almighty and omniscient, as benevolent, and finally as loving; nor from a sense of God immanent and pervading, yet transcending all that He inspires or directs. And certainly it should not be regarded as springing from the sense of beauty, and the endeavour to incorporate the full consideration of humanity in imaginative literature and the sister arts. For these, like other manifestations of the mind, are quite as much the exponent as the means of progress.

From no one of these phases of human faculty, impulse, or endeavour has arisen the wonderful, though chequered and unsteady, progress and achievement of mankind. The teaching of history is that all human faculties have made their contributions; have shown themselves beneficent factors in the general advance, or occasionally less apt and fortunate. We have the whole nature of man, and every side of it, to thank or execrate for the heights on which we find ourselves and for the precipices lying before us.

Assuredly then, by virtue of their contribution to the progress of mankind, these phases or faculties of human nature, and every one of them, are valid factors in human progress, and severally representative of its principles and truth. Each one has extended in some direction the horizon of man's vision; each one has had its share in building the huge monument, or many monuments, of human experience and knowledge. Since they have so far proved valid instruments in the realization of man's destinies, how are we justified in withdrawing our credence from some of them and swearing an exclusive allegiance to others ?

Even our animal instincts have been and still are part of human life, making for the fullness of its experience. So is our gregariousness, our tendency to seek the company of others, to conform to their ways, and also to regard their welfare. As the impulses of fellowship develop, they become distinctly human : they make further advance through friendship, confidence, and respect. Do we not know more from having felt friendship and a sense of trust in our fellows ? Do we not learn through love ? through love of parents, through love of wife or husband, through love of our children ? Love may make the valid content and often the constructive principle of our thinking.

And has not the sense of wonder led man on ? Wonder at all the things about him, wonder at the heavens and the eternal stars ; more intimate wonder at the unfolding of the flowers, wonder unspeakable at his fellows and himself. This wonder also is a kinetic impulse or principle in his thinking.

Then as man, partly through his wonder, constructs a scheme of things, may not his wonder grow and turn to fear and reverence, and at last

to love, of that which built the matter of his life
and vision, and set him in the midst ?   How shall
he think the plan without the planner ?   How
shall he think a planner or a doer or a maker without intelligence and will ?   Although he fears the
pains and perils of his life, how shall he look on all
the goodliness around him and within himself, and
not ascribe benevolence to the gods ?   And with
his further thought ever looking for unity, and his
heart seeking an object worthy of his entire adora-
tion, shall he not feel and think of God as supreme
and good ?   Will he not find God creative for the
reason that God loved the good, and sought its
increase ?   And when he sees the untoward things
of life, its grievous failures and its depths of wrong,
may not his faith in the good God perhaps go
further, and, in the manner of the Hebrew prophets,
conceive of God as afflicted in all the sufferings of
His people ?   A divine Saviour dying on the cross
to save men was a truly felt as well as truly reasoned
consummation of this intuition.

Man's answering love of God grows with this
wonderful conception.   It will enlarge his life, leading him on to new experiences of thought and feeling.

Now note well.   Such an enlargement has been
a way of truth, a way of veritable experience corresponding with the heights and depths of human
life.   Its value, its verity, as a true factor in the
enlargement of human life and knowledge, is not
impaired by the fact that not all men through all

time will continue to project their thought and feeling along this path, or by the means of what to them has become a symbol.

But again note well. Just as previous forms of reverent religion, and above them all, the faith in the risen Saviour of mankind, were not altogether of the reason, and yet proved valid for the enlargement of the truth of experience, so now experiences of other modes of love and reverence toward God the Creator and all-permeating cause of life are valid. And again they will represent more of the insistences of our nature than are circumscribed within sheer reason. Reason to-day is no more the exclusive vehicle of truth than it has been in the past. We must trust the whole man.

God exists; we may be as sure of Him as ever; it is only the rational proofs of God that change and lose their validity. The sense of the divine, the strength and comfort of belief in God, may still be the grandest verity of human life; may still assure us that here and forever all things shall never cease to work together for good in them that love God, who rest in the sure harmony of relationship with the divine and omniscient and omnipotent love. Not yet has truth faded from the words of Jesus in John's Gospel: this is life eternal that they should know thee the only true God—life eternal, whether, after the change called death, the individual continue or be merged in the love divine which was his source of life.

And reason, the sheer perceptive and rational intelligence—God forbid that we should impugn its vast share in all human progress, the progress of the whole man. It has been the ladder by which mankind have mounted from the dark pit of ignorance, mounted toward the light of knowledge. And we still need knowledge, and ever more knowledge. To-day, it is through the many provinces of physical research that knowledge is flooding in upon us. Open the flood-gates ! never fear. The noblest exercise of freedom is the pursuit of truth. Only hold fast to the moral sense which has been slowly built up through the ages, finally resulting in a certain precept : do unto others as you would that they should do to you—which is the precept of love, human and divine. Science, the pursuit of knowledge, in itself is gloriously human, a glorious part of the progress of the whole man. But in its application to human utilities it needs love's guidance.

On its side, love needs knowledge, and still more knowledge, that it may build out intelligently the individual life in its human relationships, and in the service which preserves society. God keep us from ignorance, and from those floods of folly which never cease to menace the continuance of human growth and welfare. Stand firm against the waves of ignorant emotion. Let us never forget that there have been periods of retrogression, and let us make our fight that ours be not one of them.

There still are saints among us, and degenerates, mental degenerates, moral degenerates. But most people are bad and good, selfish and hard, or upon occasion self-sacrificing, even self-consecrating. Often their actions are suggested by the collective dominant impulse making the spiritual air they breathe. Thus millions were impelled to sacrifice and consecration in the Great War, from which we issued somewhat unstrung, with our nerves and teeth on edge, restless and irritable, disinclined to persistent labour.

It is for us through firm resolve and patient endeavour to surmount this crisis of shaken nerves and unreasonable desires, when fools talk folly, but when the logic of fact will still shake itself out into the sure event, which will accord with the energies of men and women and the possibilities of our earth.

Through it all, love has grown; there is more love in the world to-day than ever before. One cause of the restlessness of these particular years and of the industrial conflicts pervading our communities is the dumb or outspoken conviction that every one should have at heart the welfare of the whole. Men and women are irritated, seeing others so frequently infringe this principle. Much has been learned in these last years of the ills resulting from that love of one group of persons which entails hostility to another group. And the mind is heard still urging men not to fly in the face of the impossible, and demand more than is forthcoming from the earth.

Patience is needed. The working out of the moral issue cannot but be slow, since it is so very complex. It may be single, with man and wife, or with parents and children. But as human relationships extend to larger groups, and multiply between group and group, people and people, how involved and difficult do they become! Founders of religion and philosophers have set the lines of religious and moral adjustment. It is for the peoples to work out the applications in law and conduct and the mutual accommodations of social life. The present tendency is toward a social democracy ever more insistent upon the welfare of the less favoured, the less intelligent and energetic, whose claim to well-being is the claim of need.

We have gathered the contents of the past for the broadening of the bases of our knowledge; we ourselves have added much. The upward road of intelligent endeavour lies still before; its steeps still beckon us. Be ours persistence, and endeavour, and untiring industry; with knowledge directed by love, and love guided by knowledge. Ignorance is always bad. The truth shall make you free. These words of Christ knock at the door of every heart; they enter also through the windows of the mind. They point to the blessedness of those who love and follow the truth of God.

Life confirms them—the wisdom of the ages,

and the accumulated knowledge that we now possess. Human progress still points onward through the action of the free intelligence, the righteously resolving will, and the ever more enlightened love of God and man. These joined and united spiritual elements of life make man's true well-being. They alone free him from the chains of physical law—which also may have wrought benevolently under the creative will of God. Yet the earth and all its laws is but man's matrix. The physical universe is his discipline and inspiration. His destiny is mind and freedom, and is not bound up in the earth.

There is little ground for thinking that the human race will endure upon this earth, any more or any longer than the myriad races of animals which have lived in the aeons of the past. We may be succeeded by other animals fitted to other conditions, other links in the chain of physical processes. But what of that, if in the meanwhile the race of mankind shall have accomplished its earthly destiny, which is its spiritual preparation ; through which it shall have attained the eternal freedom of the spirit. Through many conflicts and in many ways, but always in the way of freedom, the human soul has been emerging, and has been gathering, as it were, affinity to God, in whom lies its immortality.